Britannica Bookshelf - Great Lives

Putting Electrons to Work
DAVID SARNOFF

KARSH, OTTAWA

Putting Electrons to Work

DAVID SARNOFF

by John Tebbel

ENCYCLOPAEDIA BRITANNICA PRESS
Chicago New York London

For
CINDY AND JOHNNY
caretakers of the future

TABLE OF CONTENTS

Portrait of a Genius

On the remote 53rd floor of the RCA Building, behind a leather-topped desk in a handsome limed-oak office, at the center of the complex known to millions of Americans as Radio City, sits a stocky, dynamic man who has probably affected the daily lives of more Americans than any other human being. He gave them radio and television. At 72, he is planning to give them the keys to space. His name is David Sarnoff, chairman of the board of Radio Corporation of America, unquestionably the most powerful man the history of communications has ever known, a man who has made the future come true.

If it is possible he is lonely at the lofty summit of the empire he has created, it is equally true that the prospect he surveys would intimidate most other men. Sarnoff is in direct and more or less absolute control of a vast network of sound and sight that embraces the earth. There is the National Broadcasting Company, whose radio and television stations bring the world to the doorstep of the listening and watching audience of the United States. There is the RCA Victor Record Division whose records spin on millions of turntables, many of them manufactured by the company itself. RCA Laboratories are busy perfecting the old wonders and inventing new ones. RCA Communications, Inc., has more than 80 radiotelegraph circuits that send messages into every part of the world—more than 200,000,000 words a year. Its Leased Channel Service makes international teletype communication possible for stockbrokers, airlines, and thousands of merchants, domestic and international, as well as federal agencies.

RCA itself is in the manufacturing business. Its 18 plants make every kind of radio or related gadget, and television sets, phonographs, electron microscopes, and computers among other things.

Sarnoff, in brief, heads a giant corporation which is involved in show business, news gathering, advertising, manufacturing, broadcasting, patent licensing, commercial communications, and research. All told it employs about 100,000 people in its 30 American manufacturing locations and 13 others abroad, and grosses nearly $2,000,000,000 a year.

What kind of man sits at the controls of this empire, of which even Alexander could never have dreamed, and how did he get there? The answer is at once a legend and a story largely unknown to a new generation of young Americans, looking off into space and unaware that the man who provides the window they look through is the same man who brought those commonplace devices, radio and television, to their fathers and mothers.

For David Sarnoff's career has spanned the most exciting era in American life, the past half-century, when the tree of the nineteenth century industrial revolution burst into the overpowering bloom of twentieth century technology. He saw it happen; he has done as much as one man could do to make it happen. His story has been called, aptly, one of the great romances of industry, but it is more than that. It is a story unique in the chronicles of the men who made the nation, because it combines the supreme adventure of ideas with the more familiar story of business success.

Superficially the Sarnoff story is based on the old conventional rags-to-riches theme, the rise of a poor immigrant boy from the lower East Side of New York to success by dint of hard work and virtue. The General, as everyone calls Sarnoff, plainly dislikes the comparison, and with reason. Where the conventional nineteenth century version of "success" was a simple rise to wealth, Sarnoff has a different conception of the word.

"Success results when a man has the opportunity to express unimpeded the forces within him, whatever they may be," he says. "To be able to develop and enjoy these forces is the greatest measure of success. And wealth is not an evidence of success, contrary to popular opinion, nor is its possession an evidence of achievement."

Like his friend Bernard Baruch, the General does not consider himself a rich man, and he is far from having anywhere near Baruch's wealth. Baruch, whose fortune is estimated at somewhere near $25,000,000, often says—and with truth—that if he had not decided in 1912 to devote most of his time to public service, he would be a rich man today—meaning that his fortune would be three or four times greater, like those of his contemporaries who devoted themselves to making money. Similarly, Sarnoff, whose salary is reported as $200,000 a year and who lives in a style within the reach of comparatively few men, nevertheless points out that his career could have made him one of the richest men in America if wealth had been his motivation. But it was not, and never has been. He regards himself as a creator, like the inventor, the philosopher, the musician.

The General's particular creative genius is an ability to understand the abstract language of science and to translate it into devices that will benefit mankind. Understanding the nature of wireless communication, he foresaw the instruments that made radio and television universal and marshaled the scientific forces necessary to make these dreams come true, as well as the manufacturing organizations equally necessary to make them available on the marketplace. When the atom's secrets were unlocked and the doors to space were swung ajar, Sarnoff again was able to project these scientific discoveries into satellites and space exploration.

Now that the color television he pioneered has come into its own, the General's company is already in space. It was designer and developer of the Federal government's Tiros weather satellite, and chief contractor for communications satellite, Project Relay. On earth, Sarnoff has large dreams for linking every human being to every other with personal sight-and-sound.

The dreamer of these dreams has a right to be heard when he talks about the future. His record is illuminated by a long history of "firsts." Sarnoff proposed radio as a home instrument as early as 1916. Six years later he was arranging the first radio broadcast to a mass audience, the heavyweight championship fight between Jack Dempsey and Georges Carpentier in 1921. He made NBC the nation's first broadcasting network in 1926; and he himself made the first commercial telecast, at the opening of the New York World's Fair in 1939. He pioneered the first commercial color television sets and programs in 1954, and only six years after that he was overseeing the development of Tiros.

Outside the industry he has been an adviser to three Presidents, and performed numerous services for the government. *Time* has called him "one of the most imaginative strategists of the cold war," and leaders in many fields beat a path to his office door. Universities shower him with honorary degrees, and he could make a public speech every night in the year if he liked. "About the only honor left for General Sarnoff," Dr. Ralph Sockman, the noted New York clergyman, once observed, "is election to the Hall of Fame—and the only reason he hasn't achieved that is the stipulation that candidates must have been deceased for at least 25 years."

Behind all these visible evidences of power and achievement is an extraordinary human being. Physically, he radiates the tremendous energy which makes the careers of most successful men possible. His stocky five-foot-eight frame exudes authority and assurance. He speaks, at least during business hours, in what the Army would call the voice of command, brisk and almost harsh, coloring warmly with enthusiasm when he talks about something near his heart. Angry, he is cold and remote, with an immense, chilling reserve twice as frightening as an explosive fit of temper. His blue eyes are sharp and penetrating. His mind moves twice as quickly as most people's. He is the epitome of confidence.

A man who has been in command for more than a half-century is likely to be somewhat remote from the day-by-day business going on around him, and it is true that Sarnoff lives in a different world. It is a world characterized by plan and order, of which his immaculate desk is a symbol. He deals with one set of problems at a time, and when the papers representing it are no longer needed, they are whisked away and the desk is clear for a new batch. Thus his work never piles up.

Sarnoff with an interviewer in his office, 1961

Where most business managers dictate in a steady stream of letters and memoranda, Sarnoff seldom turns out more than a half-dozen letters in a day. The office rule is that memos written to him by subordinates must be no more than a page long, but he expresses freely whatever he has on his own mind, even if it takes 30 pages to do it. These memos are not offhand products. The General has collected what he considers the best of his memos and has had them bound in gold-tooled leather.

Disorder is his enemy. "I don't make my mind a wastepaper basket," he says. "Another thing, I don't like to see a lot of agitation around. I want to have things done in a calm, businesslike way. The other night I saw some movie drama or other that had to do with business; you should have seen the businessmen in it—picking up this phone, picking up that phone till the place looked like a madhouse. Why, I think if I had an executive like that working for me up here, I'd fire him."

There are no executives "like that" in the RCA suites nestled together in wall-to-wall carpeted dignity on the 52nd and 53rd floors of the RCA tower. It is a place of almost abnormal quiet, considering that this empire has its own quota of daily crises, like any other business. Everyone, even those who have never seen him, is conscious of the man on the 53rd floor who hates disorder.

Power may be the keynote of Sarnoff's personality, but power itself has never been the end in view. The

General has spent his life surmounting obstacles, from his earliest days. Sometimes the struggle has been the result of hard necessity, but more often it has been the natural habit of a man who enjoys taking on difficult problems and ideas. He is not particularly interested in money as money, or power as power. What interests him is everlastingly pushing hard at the barriers that separate men from what they want to achieve, whether it is the creation of a business enterprise or a new harnessing of natural forces.

If there is a common denominator among successful men, it is their total absorption in work to the exclusion of nearly everything else, and this is true of Sarnoff. His hobbies are music, reading, and boating; he doesn't play golf, and in fact has no time for games of any variety. Even at home it is not unusual for him to come in at midnight and work half the night.

He is constantly in touch with his communications empire, no matter where he may be. In the private barbership on the top floor of his home—being barbered is one of his few relaxations—there is a radio and telephone beside the chair, as there is in the barbershop adjoining his office, which is reached through a concealed door in the oak paneling. His air-conditioned Cadillac, in which his chauffeur transports him about the city, has a radiotelephone set through which he can communicate with nearly any point in the civilized world.

There is a television set in his office, as there is in the office of every other RCA executive, and when he goes to lunch in his private dining room on the floor below, down a private stairway, he has available a really impressive link to the world. A drawer in the dining table at his place contains a complicated control panel of buttons, switches, and dials. Manipulated by the General, it first agitates an innocuous looking oil painting depicting a pastoral scene of rural delights beside a waterfall, opposite his place, and causes this tranquility to slide down inside its gilt frame, disclosing a television screen of formidable proportions. The General is then able to dial any program he wants to see, including those being rehearsed in NBC's studios. He takes a paternal pride in this gadget and allows an occasional visitor to operate it.

But it is no tycoon's toy. Sarnoff could explain, to anyone who asked, exactly how the whole thing works. His understanding of complex electronic systems even now amazes some of those who work for him, particularly those who know that he had virtually no formal training in this field. Yet he understands and deals with the most difficult problems in electronics, and is well able to explain them to other people.

The electron, the earliest discovered of the smallest particles of matter, came into man's consciousness about the time Sarnoff was born, as he is fond of noting, and its uses have been the substance of the General's life. How its awesome properties have woven together the separate parts of his life are dramatically illustrated by two devices in his office. There, in a glass case, is mounted

Sarnoff using the telegraph key on his desk

the wireless key that the 19-year-old Sarnoff operated for 72 historic hours when the liner *Titanic* sank in 1912, an episode that was a major turning point in his life. In a desk drawer is a silver-plated telegraph key that the director of the RCA empire could use, if he chose, to put himself in instant contact with the radio stations and studios he controls.

In reality, of course, he would be unlikely to do so. The key is a symbol. To perform the business of conducting RCA's worldwide organization, Sarnoff has developed one of the most efficient managerial systems in American business, born of the passion for such efficiency which controls his own activities. "I don't want to do what someone else can do," he says, and so confines himself largely to policy matters when he sits at his clean and massive desk. Like any first-class executive, he knows how to delegate authority. Papers flow from his desk marked "PSM," for "Please see me," or "Pls handle," or often merely a succinct "Yes!" or "No!" Speeches are a different matter. He works on them himself, sometimes through a dozen or more drafts, before he scrawls "*stet*" (the printer's mark meaning "let it stand") across the first page. This mark usually does not go on a speech until he has tried it out on his wife Lizette at home.

Business as business is only one aspect of the General's life, but it is something for which he has demonstrated remarkable talent. When he became president of RCA in 1930, there were few who envied him. The radio industry had been struck a staggering blow by the Depression, and RCA's income had plummeted from $182,000,000 in 1929 to a slim $62,000,000 by 1933. In addition, a government antitrust action concerning the Company was settled in 1932, as a result of which General Electric and Westinghouse agreed to dispose of their stock interests in RCA.

Another man coming into the presidency at so precarious a time might have trimmed sail and considered himself lucky to ride out the storm. Not Sarnoff. Boldly he pushed ahead with expensive and expansive research programs. Meanwhile, he steered the corporation so skillfully that it paid its first dividend in 1937, and since that time has never shown a deficit. Today it is the 25th largest company in America.

A recent example of the indomitable Sarnoff at work was the fight over color television, which came to a climax in 1950. When this struggle began, RCA went into the battle with considerable reluctance. It had been developing its own system, one which would operate in the standard black-and-white channels and would therefore be "compatible," meaning that the color picture could also be received in black-and-white by those who did not have color sets, a highly important element in building an audience. The Columbia Broadcasting System, on the other hand, was ready to demonstrate a noncompatible system.

Sarnoff wanted to wait for a test between these systems until his own was thoroughly tested, but the Federal

[23]

Communications Commission was anxious to approve standards for the industry so that the new development in television would become commercially feasible as soon as possible. Knowing that the Commission did not intend to wait, Sarnoff ordered the research placed on a crash basis, and in April 1950 he took a characteristic gamble by demonstrating the RCA system before the FCC, hoping he could convince them to wait, if not actually to approve the compatible technique.

His doubts and anxieties proved to be correct. There was nothing wrong with the basic system; it is the same one employed in all color sets today. In 1950, however, it was not ready. Sarnoff summarized his demmonstration wryly: "The monkeys were green, the bananas were blue, and everyone had a good laugh." Soon after, the FCC approved CBS's non-compatible system, which was producing a good picture.

The disadvantages in producing such a color set were nevertheless so obvious that CBS wisely decided not to take advantage of the decision and try to market its system. Then the Korean War curtailed research and development sharply, thus postponing a final decision. While the war went on, Sarnoff went ahead quietly with all the facilities available to him, pushing his research men to iron out the wrinkles in the compatible system. When the war was over, the FCC reversed itself and set up new color standards recommended to it by a committee from the whole industry. No one was astonished that these new standards were substantially those

Sarnoff had advocated from the beginning of the controversy.

The General is a bold and persevering fighter for whatever he advocates, and it is characteristic of his pioneering efforts that he has never hesitated to spend his company's money if he believed that whatever he was doing with it would pay off eventually. In the Depression, for example, justifying his undiminished research program, he declared that troubled times called for "brave dollars" as well as brave men. In developing black-and-white television, he poured out $50,000,000 before the new medium earned back a penny, and he spent nearly three times that much on color. Presently he has staked a fortune on the development of computers, forthrightly entering a field already dominated by International Business Machines, and he is pushing to circle the globe with color television by satellite. "The future has always interested me more than the past," the General remarks succinctly.

The Sarnoff that the world and his business associates see is a dominant, determined man, vigorous and commanding, superbly talented in a half-dozen directions and intensely involved with the whole immense empire he controls. *Fortune,* the magazine of business, has summarized him: "He is a whole cast of characters —the dramatis personae of a long play about success in American business. He is at once a farsighted leader and a volatile boss; a charmer and a hardboiled taskmaster; a philosopher ('competition brings out the best in products and the worst in men') but withal a fearful competitor himself. . . ."

There is, quite naturally, another Sarnoff, one seen in off guard moments during the business day and by his wife and his few intimates at home. A man of the General's particular personality does not easily inspire anecdotes, and there are few to be heard in the RCA tower, but those that exist are revealing.

John B. Kennedy, the radio commentator, recalled several years ago a day in Atlantic City when Sarnoff and his late brother Irving, a man who was prominent in the New York radio retailing business, were talking with a group of radio dealers. The General, his cigar cocked at a militant angle, was needling his younger brother in the manner of older brothers everywhere in the world.

"Quit riding me," Irving said, with mock anger. "You quit riding me or I'll tell mother."

Sarnoff walked away smiling, sharing Irving's quiet enjoyment of the fact that their capable mother had dominated all four of the Sarnoff boys.

The General relaxes most, perhaps, with music and musicians. Next to science and business, they are his nearest and dearest interests. His closest friends, aside from Baruch, the late Albert Lasker, and the late Herbert Bayard Swope (a trio once referred to as Sarnoff's "kitchen cabinet") have been musicians. One is Samuel Chotzinoff, music director of NBC and the man who made the NBC Opera Company a national television institution. Another is the violin virtuoso Jascha Heifetz. The pianist Artur Rubinstein is still another.

When he was alive, Maestro Arturo Toscanini became one of Sarnoff's good friends, a relationship surprising to some people who could not understand what these utterly different men had in common. They had, of course, the NBC Symphony, still active today as the Symphony of the Air, a first-rank orchestra that Sarnoff had especially created for the distinguished conductor. That would have been enough in itself, perhaps, but the two men had a shared interest in what was going on in the world, as well as in the special world of music. Sarnoff introduced the Maestro to television, which he had avoided, and was delighted when Toscanini became an avid sports follower, particularly of the fights. If the Sarnoffs—or anyone else—came to dinner on a fight night, dinner had to be early and over with before the slugging began.

Once, however, the relationship was unexpectedly strained when the Sarnoffs entertained by giving a surprise party for Toscanini. It was a surprise, but to the temperamental maestro, not entertaining. Shown up to the sixth floor of Sarnoff's house when he arrived, he was disconcerted when he was asked whether he had a reservation, and further disturbed to be ushered into an upstairs room that had been turned into a nightclub for the occasion. Jazz greeted his affronted ears, and he could scarcely believe it when he saw his friend Sarnoff dressed as a ringmaster introducing circus acts, in which the General's celebrated friends were the stars. Astounded and horrified, Toscanini watched Heifetz's sister Elza, the wife of playwright S. N. Behrman, riding a make-believe horse. Then he put his head in his hands and would look at the show no more.

The General and his friends were not discouraged. They went on to other imaginative parties, at one of which, on Sarnoff's birthday, Chotzinoff impersonated him in a most un-Sarnofflike fashion, sitting at a breakfast table and talking into a half-dozen telephones at once while he beat the table with his fist and chewed cigars. Unlike Toscanini, Sarnoff was delighted.

Alone in his 30-room house on East Seventy-first Street with Lizette, the General comes as close to the rest of humanity as a man with his background and in his position can come. It is not, obviously, the kind of dwelling most men could call home, with its six floors, two patios, barbershop, projection room, and a profusion of television and radio sets, but in it the General leads a life as near to normal as possible.

He has, as his wife explains, "his crotchets." For one thing, he hates to tip—not out of any penuriousness but simply because the act of tipping embarrasses him as a human transaction. Consequently he will leave his hat in the car rather than check it; and when he eats out, it is usually at a restaurant on a small, select list. The people who serve him in these places are tipped once a year by check, along with his barber and manicurist. Their wait is compensated by Sarnoff's generosity.

Through this system he believes that he is maintaining some sense of dignity between the server and the served.

Years ago he was persuaded to give up driving, a change accomplished when he had a mobile radiotelephone installed in his car. In his driving days it was always a contest between driver and machine. "I used to sit beside him, uncomfortable," his wife has recalled, "wondering whether I ought to tell the master of the electronic age that I did not like the way he took the last corner."

At home he ranges over the six floors of the house, from a small study on the first to his own office on the fourth (the entire fourth floor is his personal domain) to the sixth, where there is a solarium and a terrace—and the barbershop. Sunday morning in the barbershop is a Sarnoff institution. His friend Sam the Barber, who has shaved him for nearly 20 years, ministers not only to him but usually to three or four old friends who drop in. Afterward the men eat brunch together and spend the afternoon talking.

Sometimes the house seems more like a laboratory than a home to his wife, when she contemplates the electronic devices that decorate it from top to bottom. There may be as many as 20 television sets scattered through the house at one time, nearly all of them experimental models in various stages of development. They are constantly replaced as new developments come along. "I just about learn to work one when it's gone," Mrs. Sarnoff complains gently.

[29]

The General's study desk is equipped with a battery of buttons that control the room lights, operate the radio, and make a painting disappear in favor of a television screen, as in his RCA dining room. A similar panel is built into a corner of his bed. Sarnoff thinks it is silly to do anything by hand that electricity can do. There is, in fact, a professional panel room that controls the entire intricate system of radio and television throughout the house, but not including the fully equipped sound-movie projection room in the library. The drawing room, which is decorated with Chinese murals, is large enough to hold a small concert audience, and often does.

Aside from the barbershop, Sarnoff's favorite room is his fourth-floor office, which is weighted down with a vast collection of ribbons, medals, citations, plaques, trophies, autographed portraits, a small library of press clippings and speeches bound in gold-tooled leather, and 41 volumes of notes for a history of his life and times, which he has said he will not permit to be published until after his death.

In this spacious, somewhat incredible house, Sarnoff has seen his three sons grow up—one of them, Robert, to be chairman of the board of NBC. The growing up process brought the usual quota of juvenile problems to the attention of the man who so much dislikes trivia. Once his youngest son, Tom, fell in love with a white terrier in a Madison Avenue pet shop and yearned to take him home, where no dogs had been permitted on the theory that they required country fields, not city houses.

Tom wrote to his father: "Dear Dad, I have just seen the most beautiful dog. I would love to have him for my birthday. I could teach him tricks. If you get me the dog, I promise that the first trick I will teach him is to stay out of your way." When the General read this note, he went to the pet shop himself and bought the dog that proved to be the forerunner of other dogs, alligators, birds, and guppies. As a father, Sarnoff drew the line only at a pair of wallabies sent to Tom by an Australian admirer of his father. These animals went to the Central Park Zoo.

Sarnoff has always been a family man, to an extent the schedule of a busy industrialist seldom permits. He loves, for example, to conduct the traditional ceremonies of the Jewish year, most of which celebrate the family in love and gratitude.

As far as the usual problems of humanity are concerned, the General is not exceptional. He tends to be overweight, and his battle against the calories is complicated by his dislike of sports and physical exercise. He has dutifully tried such pleasures as horseback riding in Central Park, but his wife recalls that in his brief riding period he would go to the window, look out with satisfaction on a rainy morning, and remark, "Thank goodness, I don't have to ride today." He has also tried fishing, with an equal lack of enthusiasm for that popular sport.

[31]

He does not drink, except for an occasional glass of wine, but his big black cigars are a trademark. When he is not smoking them, in his familiar black holder, he has a pipe in his mouth. He told Winston Churchill, presenting him with a gift of cigars: "The only thing in which I can keep up with you is smoking."

According to his wife, he likes any kind of food "as long as it is fattening," particularly the kind of Old World dishes his mother made, such as pot roast and potato pancakes, loaded with calories. Only his breakfast is Spartan—a slice of toast and a little fruit. He would like more, but Mrs. Sarnoff, guarding his weight, prevents it unless the servants sneak him a roll, to which he may add a little jelly he steals himself. "When we are riding to the theatre, or to a friend's house," his wife says, "he will often ask, 'Do you have any candy?' I keep hard candies for him in a box in my purse."

His love for gadgets is like a small boy's. He has every possible kind of pocket tool, and a basement workshop full of larger items. His drawers are full of pens, pencils, and similar everyday working equipment, from which he chooses in the morning as he does his ties. RCA built a special transistor radio for him that he carries in his vest pocket. The set is equipped with earphones so that he can listen to a program even during a waiting period at a public banquet. At one such affair he jokingly remarked to a lady guest that he used the earphones only when he was bored by a dinner companion, then absently plugged them in a little later

[32]

before he noticed that the same lady was seated next to him. His agile brain produced a saving response. Turning over the earphones and set to the lady, he remarked, "It's yours—if you're bored by me, you can use this."

No one is known to be bored with Sarnoff's conversation. At the beach, at home, anywhere, he will talk about science, or the arts, or industry, or communications, to anyone who will listen. His wife has often seen him at the beach in a pair of swimming trunks, talking at first to a stranger but soon surrounded by a circle of other people who sit entranced while he talks and answers questions—usually about developments of the future.

At home he enjoys equally talking at the small dinner parties his wife arranges to provide him with intellectual stimulation. He hates to go out. "He would rather eat two soft-boiled eggs at his own table than go to any restaurant," Mrs. Sarnoff says. But with congenial guests in his own house, he relaxes completely and speaks with the energy, enthusiasm, and charm his friends know so well. He likes to talk about foreign affairs, politics, economics, and such subjects, but always the conversation turns in time to science, electronics—and the future. Then, as his wife says, "We are all sitting on the edges of our chairs, looking with him into the unknown."

A day in the life of Sarnoff begins at seven-thirty when a masseur comes to his house and gives him a massage before breakfast. He and his wife do not breakfast together—he eats alone downstairs; she has hers in her room—but even at this early hour he is the communications expert in action, sending up clippings from the morning paper for her to see, reading messages she sends down to him. Before he leaves the house, Mrs. Sarnoff comes down, examines his necktie, and kisses him good-bye, like any suburban housewife.

Then, during the day, he is the man behind the desk in the RCA tower, smoking his cigars, dealing methodically with one problem at a time, sometimes thinking and planning by himself with his head in the stars.

At six he comes home from the office, and his first words are invariably, "Is Mrs. Sarnoff home?" He never fails to telephone if he is going to be late, a virtue most wives would particularly admire. As soon as he is home, the General goes to bed and sleeps soundly for about an hour and a half until dinner is ready. If he is particularly tired and sleeps longer, Mrs. Sarnoff lets the servants go and gets dinner herself, which she did for years before the family had servants.

The house runs according to his schedule, and he is never made to accomodate himself. When his wife senses that he has worked too hard and needs rest, a conclusion she comes to by wifely radar, she tactfully cancels whatever has been planned for the evening. One certain sign of overexertion is his appetite; he eats more when he is under great pressure or has particularly difficult problems. But he snaps back quickly, sometimes with no more help than a 15-minute nap.

Sarnoff is not a man who runs by the clock. When he comes home as late as one o'clock, he may feel like working in his office. If his wife is tempted to behave like a wife and urge him to go to bed, she restrains herself. "Who knows what new idea or new development is taking shape in his mind?" she says. "Do I want to go down in history as the woman who kept some important scientific advance from taking place because she was sleepy?" Consequently she sits up with him, reading while he works, listening if he produces a new idea he wants to talk about.

On occasion, at three in the morning, he has been known to say suddenly, "Let's clean out." Mrs. Sarnoff knows what that means. It happens three or four times a year. They go through his suits, socks, shirts, and ties and make a pile to give away. Cleaning out is about as close as the General comes to a hobby. But he finds it difficult to give away shoes, which are one of his special enthusiasms. Otherwise, he is undemanding about clothes. Mrs. Sarnoff helps him pick out his suits and prevents him from buying the same ones—plain blue, or gray, or brown.

Giving away clothes is the smallest part of his charities. Not only does he contribute to the usual public funds, but he is the kind of philanthropist who unobtrusively sends young students through college and gives money to revolving loan funds at schools. He is a trustee of several colleges and universities, including such institutions as Pratt Institute, and the Educational

Alliance, where he first went to school. Nor is his only philanthropy in education and the funds. Old friends from the lower East Side have known his benefactions with gratitude, and the East Side itself has seen him on occasion, when he returns to the old neighborhood, sees the familiar scenes once more, and talks with the few onetime cronies who remain.

All these facets of personality are his points of contact with the everyday world. The inner world of dreams and plans, in which he has spent so much productive time, shows itself in odd ways. One is his dislike of being interrupted, which a casual observer might put down to ego, but which in reality derives from Sarnoff's respect for orderly thinking. He himself never interrupts anyone. But whether talking or listening, those closest to him are aware of his ability to shift his mental gears and transport himself to the inner world, where he only appears to be listening, and where his conversation is mechanically responsive. His wife has seen him talking on the telephone for nearly an hour, listening to the man at the other end without a word while he is busy with his own thoughts.

Who is the real Sarnoff? one might ask. Is it the figure of command in the RCA office who says briskly when someone asks him which part of the corporation is his favorite, "The one that's in trouble. If things are going all right, they don't hear anything from me"? Or is it the quiet man at home in his "upstairs office," in the house where he has lived for more than three decades, looking up now and then at the inscribed portraits of Presidents Roosevelt, Truman, and Eisenhower on the wall, or the bronze plaque of Marconi, or the musical birthday tribute from Toscanini, or the bookshelves packed with autographed first editions, or "the hardware you collect in the course of a lifetime," as he refers to his citations, plaques, trophies, ribbons, and medals—or, most fondly, the World War II pictures of his three sons in uniform, and his wife in the uniform of a Red Cross nurses' aide? Often he opens the albums that record the lives of the eight Sarnoff grandchildren from cradle to college.

The real Sarnoff is all these men and more. He is the true product of the exciting times that have made him, and of a life that is an incredible story from beginning to end, one that could have happened only in America.

Chapter 2

A Boy Comes to America

No career ever began under less auspicious circumstances than David Sarnoff's. When he was born, on February 27, 1891, he was about as far from a position of power and influence in the world as an infant could be, both geographically and economically. His birthplace was a bleak village named Uzlian, on the steppes of southern Russia, and his family were desperately poor.

In the little town, where no more than 200 people lived, there were no upper and lower classes, only degrees of poverty. Most of the villagers were Jews, whose houses were small wooden shacks and whose food came principally from the scraggly gardens behind these dwellings. Money was scarcely known in this remote region, which was several hours away from the nearest city, Minsk.

Trading had replaced the usual commercial life in Uzlian's primitive society, and most of the townsmen, like David's father, were traders. They went about among the neighboring peasants on the steppes, bartering shoes, clothing, and similar necessities for produce and, if they were lucky, livestock. It was a precarious life. The struggle was to stay alive, to get a minimum of food and clothing. Most hoped for nothing more.

David's father, Abraham, was different. Like the others, he heard the travelers' tales about America that reached even this isolated spot, but he did not sigh and consign the Land of Promise to the realm of impossible dreams. Instead, he began to plan how he might achieve what must have seemed virtually impossible—to transport himself and his family from the lonely, hopeless village to the glories and riches of New York.

By the time David was four years old, his father had made his decision. He would sell all his trader's stock, leave enough to keep the family alive for a time, and buy a steerage ticket to America with the remainder. In its own way, it was as bold a gamble as his son would take many years later in the world of high corporation finance.

The parting was agonizing, and it would not have been surprising if some village tongues wagged about this man Sarnoff who would leave his family and go off to America by himself. No one could be certain if he would even get there, much less be able to earn enough in a strange country to keep on supporting the family and save the sum required to bring them over. But the mother was brave and willing to take the chance, although she would be left with David, another son even younger, and a third still unborn.

The family parted with tears and promises. David's mother, who was the descendant of a long line of rabbis, decided soon after that she could make her own hard life alone more tolerable and at the same time fulfill the dream she had for her son by sending him to his granduncle, a rabbi who ministered to a settlement even smaller than Uzlian, a village called Korme, where the good rabbi's flock numbered only 12 families.

When David was five, his mother knew it was time for him to go to Korme. By now her husband's letters, bravely optimistic but more than ever vague about when he could send for his family, had convinced her that life in the New World had not proved to be the quick road to fortune they had dreamed of. The elder Sarnoff was working and saving, but life in New York was as hard as it had been at home. It would take time. Meanwhile, the mother reasoned, David was the proper age to begin his training as a rabbi, and the granduncle was the proper person; in spite of his humble station, he was known to be deeply versed in the Jewish religion.

Now there were more tears as the mother kissed her firstborn goodbye. There would be one less mouth to feed, but it was a mouth and a son she could hardly bear to send on such a long journey. Korme was some

500 miles away. Only her proud hope that he would one day be a rabbi made the parting less intolerable.

As for David, he was already homesick but nevertheless excited by this first great adventure of his life. The excitement was enough to sustain him while he traveled by train from Minsk to the railway station nearest Korme. But then he was tumbled into what the operators were pleased to call a "stage," which was no more than a rough country cart, its bottom covered with a thin layer of straw. On this David and a few other hardy travelers huddled together while the cart creaked and bounced over roads that were scarcely passable, 200 miles through a dreary, rolling plains country until it stopped at last at the village of Korme, clinging to a hillside.

Here was a desolation he had not known even in Uzlian. At least he had enjoyed a few playmates in his native village, but in Korme he was the only child in the settlement. His granduncle was a kind man, but stern and severely orthodox; if David was going to be a rabbi, his granduncle meant to have no nonsense about it. The boy would have to learn 2,000 words of the Talmud, a book of Jewish traditions, every day, as well as sit for his regular religious lessons. So began a harsh regime that lasted nearly four years. David rose at dawn and began his Talmudic studies at seven. They went on all day, with time out only for meals, until eight o'clock at night. He had no playmates, no recreation, no relief from grinding study.

[42]

How welcome the news must have been, between his ninth and tenth birthdays, when his mother wrote and told him to come home. Abraham Sarnoff had at last sent them the money to come to America. They would leave as soon as David arrived. He departed from Korme without tears.

It was arranged that he would join his mother and his two brothers in Minsk, where they would all take the train to Libau, Latvia, the first port of embarkation. "The hour that followed our reunion in Minsk," Sarnoff wrote years later, "is etched in my memory so deeply that I shall never forget one detail. We were waiting until it was time to board the train for Libau when we noticed that a tremendous crowd had collected in the principal street. One of the sporadic Russian revolutions was brewing.

"As we watched the surging people, a company of mounted Cossacks came charging down. They called on the crowd to disperse. No one moved. The Cossack leader barked a word of command—and the whole company rode into the wailing mob, lashing out with their long whips and trampling women and children under the hooves of their horses. The sight sickened me and I clung to my mother's skirts."

His departure from the Old World could not have been more symbolic, nor could the promise of the New World have seemed more bright.

"A day later," Sarnoff continued, "we were on the boat, the first I had ever seen. I marveled at its movement as it swept out of the harbor, and all the rest of the day and long after the stars came out at night, I watched the receding shore line and the other vessels coming and going."

After a short voyage, the Sarnoffs found themselves in the noisy confusion of the docks at Liverpool, England, where they were to take another ship, which loomed up awesomely large to the small boy. As the little family clung together on a corner near the pier, waiting to board, a trolley car clanged down the street —another first sight for them. "To me it seemed moving without any kind of propelling force," Sarnoff recalled, "and I was sure that everyone in America must travel about in that fashion. I suppose we were as strange a sight to other people as the trolley was to me. In Russia it is still cold in early June, and we were wearing the fur caps and clothing that were a suitable enough garb when we left home."

They were no more than safely aboard the steamer, as steerage passengers bound for Montreal, when David had the greatest fright of his life. His mother had brought along two large bundles, one holding the feather ticks that had been stretched on the family's board pallets at home, the other containing food enough for the whole trip. The feather ticks were the result of a mistaken notion that they could not be replaced in America, but the food—bread, cake, and pickled meats —was absolutely essential because it was kosher. David's mother had warned the boys that if anything

[44]

happened to that food, the family would not be able to eat at all. With his religious training still fresh in his mind, David knew his mother would starve rather than touch the regular steerage fare, and he himself would have accepted the same fate without questioning.

His horror is easy to imagine, then, when he saw the ticks and the straw hamper of food disappearing with a heap of baggage being lowered into the hold. A vision of starvation flashed before him, and instinctively he ran forward, leaped wildly, and plunged down into the hold after the food hamper. It was a sheer drop of 50 feet to the bottom. Fortunately, he landed on some soft bundles that broke his fall.

"Crawling around until I had found the hamper," he remembered later, "I clutched it with a death grip. Meanwhile, I could hear far-off wails from above. Mother and the other women nearby were sure that I was killed. Finally a seaman appeared, knotted a rope around my waist, and I was hoisted up like a sack of meal. I reached daylight again, holding for dear life to the basket of food."

One of the sailors watched this scene with amusement and admiration. "You'll get along all right in America," he assured David, in Russian, making one of the most conservative prophecies of the century.

The boat was small and slow, and it was nearly a month before it deposited them in Montreal. There the family took the train again, to Albany, where they boarded the night boat for New York and landed on a sultry July morning in the fabled metropolis. The year was 1900.

"I had my first look at my adopted country from the deck of a Hudson River steamer," Sarnoff recalls. "Manhattan's skyscrapers, including the fabulous 29-story Park Row Building, then the tallest office structure in the world, sparkled in the morning sun. The harbor was crammed with shipping. The people on the pier looked happy, purposeful, prosperous. 'Here, indeed,' I thought, 'is the land of promise.' Two days later I was peddling papers on the streets of this land of promise to help support my family, but I was full of hope. I was unable to speak or understand a word of English, but I was in a new world, a new society, among a new people."

At the pier there occurred one of those mixups common among immigrants and their families in those days. As the Sarnoffs anxiously scanned the dock for the first sight of father Abraham, whom they had not seen for six long years, and whom the youngest boy had never seen at all, they could not find his familiar, bearded face among the people milling about in the confusion of the pier. He had gone to the wrong pier to wait for them.

Bewildered and alone in the clanging swirl of New York traffic, terrified by the crowds and the noise and the overwhelming impact of the city, the mother appealed to a policeman, who found an interpreter and straightened matters out. They were sent to a small

[46]

boardinghouse, where Abraham soon found them and the family was tearfully and thankfully reunited.

David's mother must have had a cruel shock when she saw her husband again. The bitter struggle to keep himself alive, send money home, and still save enough to bring his family to America had been successful, but it had shattered his health. The asthma that had troubled him for years was now chronic, and it was aggravated by his trade of house painting. It would be only a few months before he would have to take to his bed and live out the remaining years of his life as an invalid.

Meanwhile, established in the new home, a small tenement flat in the Lower East Side ghetto, David wasted no time getting a job to help support the family. He had, in fact, two jobs. No more than a day or two after his arrival he was working for $1.50 a week as a butcher's delivery boy and soon he had a paper route in the bargain.

It was a strange new world he found himself in, unbelievably removed from the monastic quiet and discipline of his granduncle's house and the simple village life of Russia. Life on the Lower East Side seethed and rumbled and groaned, laughed and cried, half in the streets and half in the crowded, hot tenements. There was struggle here, too, of the same kind he had always known. These people were poor immigrants like himself, all seeking their fortunes in the land of promise, and pushing, striving, sweating meanwhile to survive. Pushcarts and sweatshops were the hallmarks of their

[47]

aspirations. Saloons and settlement houses were their enjoyments. Yet some of them had already climbed the ladder and gone uptown to live in fine houses. Every day the neighborhood heard of some new success, a boy who had grown up on the fire escapes and in the street jungles, yet had risen to wealth and influence and a comfortable life. Anyone, they believed, could do it.

Young David was totally undismayed by the struggle before him. On the contrary, he was exhilarated by the freedom from everything he had known, which had only stifled him; he welcomed joyously the chance to work in this enchanted new land. Everything he saw and heard only stimulated him the more. Most of all he was excited about the opportunity he had to go to school. There had been no free school in Russia.

That September he entered a school building for the first time in his life. It was the Educational Alliance, on East Broadway, where immigrants were taught the English language, and where he would one day be an honorary trustee.

He had been in school about a week when the teacher told him that he was already proficient enough in the language to recite at the next school assembly. The subject assigned him was, "Cleanliness is next to godliness." Confident until the moment he stood up, poor David found his mind a blank as he faced the tittering audience; he balanced first on one foot then the other. Nothing at all would come, and the teacher had to take him to his seat.

[48]

Young Sarnoff never forgot the humiliation of that experience. It made him determined never to repeat it, and as a first step, he joined the school's debating society. Only a year later he was on the same platform, arguing clearly and forcefully the question of the day: "Resolved, that the Philippines be given their independence." It was an early training that helped him further when he became an executive, invited to speak everywhere in the world. In time he became one of the most sought after speakers in America, getting several hundred invitations a year. He wisely accepts fewer than a half-dozen.

School was only a part of David's long day. Every morning he got up at four o'clock to deliver his papers before he started off for class; then after school he was hard at work again as a delivery boy until it was time for evening study. But already a young business man, he was ready to expand in two years, when he was only 11.

A friend had told him about a newsstand for sale at Forty-sixth Street and Tenth Avenue, in the notorious Hell's Kitchen district. The stand was owned by a German who catered to a predominantly Irish clientele in this uptown slum, where crime was the order of the day but people apparently read newspapers, because the stand was profitable. The owner wanted $200 for his property. David talked it over with some of the family's neighbors, who had marked him as a boy who was likely to go far. When he went among them to borrow the money he needed for his stand, he found them not unreluctant to invest and soon he was the owner of his first enterprise.

He had also found another way to supplement his income. Finding himself in possession of a pleasant boy soprano's voice, he hired out to sing in a synagogue choir for $1.50 a week, and occasionally he appeared as soloist at weddings. Now he had a day's schedule that would make his later calendar as a corporation executive look easy. He was up at four and working with his deliveries until school, then afternoon deliveries after school until it was time for a late supper, after which he traveled by streetcar down to the Lower East Side for choir rehearsals. Sometimes it was after midnight before he got home—and there was still school work that he had to do.

Another boy might have begrudged the time at school and given up his education, but Sarnoff was fascinated by the world of the mind opening up to him. He was learning about the meaning of America, about the wonders of the universe, and his restless, active mind absorbed it all eagerly. He was especially attracted to the story of Abraham Lincoln. Here was a boy like himself, he thought, who started without money, position, or influence but who nevertheless rose to be President. "Lincoln became my inspiration," Sarnoff wrote later. "Evenings after finishing my paper route I would hurry to the public library and borrow one of the books about him. I got to know Lincoln's life better than most native Americans do. A portrait of him hangs in my office today, and another in my library at home."

It was a profit and loss time for David, these early years in America. The loss was his youth. "At ten most kids are shooting marbles," his brother Irving said later. "David never had time for marbles. All he had was work. He never had a youth." On the other hand, becoming virtually head of a family at 10, with a father too ill to work, he acquired a valuable sense of responsibility that has never left him. It made him acutely aware of responsibility, of assuming and discharging it, and quite naturally it has made him intolerant and impatient of people who will not assume it.

At 15, after six years of this hard-working routine, a minor and a major tragedy compelled him to take a new look at his life. His voice broke on the eve of the high holidays, when he would have made a considerable extra amount of money, thus ending his singing career and reducing his income, which had been no more than enough to support the family. Then his father, gasping for breath, succumbed to the asthma that had crippled him and David knew he would have to give up school and perhaps his part-time employments to look for a full-time job. There were four other children in the family, and his mother could not leave them to work.

"I didn't quite know what I was going to do," Sarnoff said later, "but I was determined that it must be something in which I could shake loose from the environments I had known. I wouldn't be a day laborer, or a dockhand, or a pushcart merchant, or a stevedore, for example.

"Before even looking for a job, I thought things over carefully. I realized that the people with whom I would have to compete in business could get a normal degree of success with a moderate amount of work. On account of my youth, however, I would have to give at least 50 per cent, perhaps 100 per cent, more effort if I expected to keep pace with them or pass them. In other words, I would have to be about twice as efficient as the other fellow. This situation did not strike me as unfair; I accepted it as a necessary handicap."

The question, however, was what the new job was to be. David had no idea where to look, but he concluded that since the one thing he knew best was selling newspapers, it was logical to go into the newspaper business; and so he went off one Saturday morning to the old New York *Herald* building at Thirty-fifth Street and Broadway to ask for a job. He was neatly dressed, optimistic, and quite unprepared for what followed.

Among the legends built up around the Sarnoff career is that he took the wrong turn in the building that morning and ended at the office of the Postal Telegraph and Commercial Cable Company instead of the *Herald's* reception desk. The truth is that he simply walked over to the first desk he saw on the main floor of the building, which happened to be the desk of Commercial Cable's manager. The company maintained a branch there, primarily for the benefit of the newspaper.

[52]

David stood for a moment until the manager looked up, meanwhile listening to the strange chatter of the telegraph equipment. It was a new song but it stirred something in him. The manager lifted his head inquiringly.

"What can I do for you?" he asked.

"I'd like to know where I can apply for a job on the *Herald*," David said.

There was something in the boy's voice and appearance—his neatness, his earnest and confident tone —that made the manager take a second look before he replied, and in that moment impelled him to deprive the *Herald* of an employee.

"How would you like to work here?" he inquired. "We need a messenger. The pay is $5 a week."

It may have been the money almost in hand, or the tantalizing sound of the key. In any case, David accepted on the spot. He had his first real job, and that day began to reach for the stars.

Chapter 3

Learning the Wireless

"**O**ne of my boys is the smartest," Sarnoff's mother used to say, "another is the kindest, a third is the handsomest. But David is lucky!"

It was a mother's fond and half-joking estimate, and there was an element of truth in it that her lucky son was the first to acknowledge. "I have never underrated the element of luck in what passes for worldly success," he once said. "I know it takes more than luck alone, but I do not hesitate to acknowledge that I have been lucky beyond my deserts. It was luck that my parents had the pioneering instinct and the good sense to bring me to this land of freedom and the opportunity that goes with freedom. It was luck that for me this opportunity materialized in an art and an industry even younger than myself. It was a lucky coincidence that I was born about the same time the electron was discovered. And it was lucky I hitched my wagon to the electron."

The hitching began on that Saturday morning when the Cable Company acquired a messenger boy and thus diverted a genius who might have flowered in the newspaper business instead. One could say it was also lucky for David Sarnoff, as well as for the millions of people he would later benefit, that the diversion took place, but what happened afterward was far from a matter of luck.

For something was already at work in the mind of this 15-year-old boy. That something was still vague and unclear, but he was aware of an enormous world to be explored and conquered. He did not yet know how he was going to do it, but he knew he wanted to reach out and touch whole areas of knowledge whose existence he only suspected. He wanted to build and plan. What? He did not know that either, but he was restless and he had visions and deep yearnings. He was eager to work, but he was aware that his need was to be in productive, creative work. He was like a young poet or painter, first conscious of his gifts and uncertain what to do with them, but wholly committed to their use.

Meanwhile, there was the Cable Company. The first thing David learned about this enterprise was that a telegraph operator earned more than an office boy. Obviously, then, the next step was to be an operator. He saved $1.50 out of his first week's salary, bought a telegraph key, and began to learn the Morse code. In most families it is the piano or violin that brings suffering. In David's, it was his telegraph key. "The noise nearly drove mother out of her mind," according to his brother Irving.

These were long days for David. He had kept his paper route, and got up as always at four in the morning. Then, after a long day at the Cable Company, he practiced the key until he could keep his eyes open no longer. But he was in a buoyant and confident mood. The time was 1906 and the air was full of promise and change, although the panic a year later would dampen enthusiasm briefly. Teddy Roosevelt was in the White House and the trusts were being busted. The muckrakers were at work on magazines and newspapers, exposing the unholy alliance between the new industrialists and the politicians.

At the moment, however, horsecars transported passengers nearly everywhere in New York, a schooner of beer cost a nickel, and a free lunch at the bar was thrown in. Gaslight flickered in houses everywhere, and a frightening gadget people called the horseless carriage snorted in the streets.

"I was only 15 years old," Sarnoff recalls, "and life for me was like a blank page—challenging and a bit frightening in its clean white emptiness."

For the first six months he was busy delivering messages and trying to learn the code. Besides practicing at home, an aspiring messenger who wanted to learn Samuel F. B. Morse's revolutionary symbols could help

[57]

himself by paying attention in the office when there were no messages to be delivered and listening to the key as the mysterious dots and dashes poured through it. David added a third element to the learning process. Having made friends with the manager from the day he went to work, he persuaded the older man to let him practice on the office instrument when there was nothing important coming over.

While he was engaged in this practicing, young Sarnoff, in the manner of telegraph operators everywhere, carried on long conversations with a man in the main offices of the company, a man he never saw. To this unseen correspondent David confided his ambition to be an operator, and one day he was rewarded when his friend told him he had heard the Marconi Company had a vacancy and advised him to apply.

At the first opportunity, Sarnoff presented himself in the headquarters of the Marconi Wireless and Telegraph Company. The man who confronted him was George S. De Sousa, the company's traffic manager, who also did the hiring.

"Could you use a man?" David asked forthrightly. "I hear you have an opening."

De Sousa looked him up and down, no doubt with some amazement. Then he addressed the applicant, who looked hardly old enough to be an office boy, in his most dignified manner.

"How old are you and what experience have you had?" De Sousa inquired.

Sarnoff told him the truth, and meanwhile a twinkle appeared in the De Sousa eye.

"I'm sorry to say we can't use a man," the manager said, when David had finished. "That job has been filled, but we *do* need a boy, an office boy, at $5.50 a week."

For a moment disappointment overwhelmed David. It was only 50 cents a week more and essentially the same job he had left, but it would be with a wireless company and the opportunity to learn more was there. He and De Sousa eyed each other while the boy hesitated, and decided they liked each other.

"I'll take it," David said.

At that moment the Marconi company was a struggling organization specializing in marine communications, with four land stations at Sea Gate, Coney Island; Sagaponack, Long Island; Siasconset, on Nantucket Island; and South Wellfleet, Massachusetts. It had only four ships with which to communicate, and it was losing money steadily.

Of this situation the new office boy knew very little at the start, but he was not long in learning. "I hated being an office boy," he said years afterward. "But because I hated it, I devised ways to make my work more interesting. One way was to read every letter I filed. My bosses didn't object, because in that way I always knew exactly where to lay my hands on any correspondence they called for. As for myself, I gained a practical education in the operation of a wireless-telegraph business. In fact, I soon became more familiar with the details of the company's work than anybody else around.

"I also took advantage of the opportunity to improve my knowledge of English. I carried a pocket dictionary, and whenever I encountered an unfamiliar word I made it a point to look it up. There was a thrill of discovery in every fresh word I learned. The president of the Marconi Company at that time was John W. Griggs, a master of forceful prose. He had been a governor of the State of New Jersey, and an attorney general of the United States. I studied his letters with special interest and tried to imitate his style."

Always, David was learning. He borrowed books on electricity, thick technical volumes, and studied them on his way to and from work. Often, worn out by the day's labor, evening study, and practice with the key, he would fall asleep in a chair and spend the night there.

At the office he soon made another discovery which added substantially to his self-acquired education. The company, he learned, was operating a small experimental shop on Front Street, where H. J. Round, leading expert of the British Marconi Company, was busy developing new transmission methods. The boy and the expert became friends, and David began to spend his Saturday afternoons and Sundays in the shop. Round was more than happy to exchange information and explanations about what he was doing for odd jobs done and other assistance given. For a boy of Sarnoff's background, it was no sacrifice to give up his day-and-a-half off.

"There were a good many executives in the office," he once explained, "but I felt no aspirations toward their jobs—at least, not through any routine office advancement. It seemed to me that the operators out in the coastal stations, and Jimmy Round down in his little shop, were nearer to the heart of radio than the men who sat in swivel chairs and gave directions. I felt that the important individual of the future would be the man who knew all about radio from practical experience. I resolved solemnly that I would become such a man."

Sarnoff was already convinced that wireless was the important invention of the day, and its development a key to unknown marvels in the future. He was determined to be in on the ground floor. In the office and the laboratory he listened breathlessly to the tales spun by wireless operators from ships who visited the office from time to time, and he read everything he could about Morse, Edison, and the scanty history of wireless.

Then came a break his mother would have called lucky. The company was asked to send two operators to an electrical show to be held for several weeks in Louisville, Kentucky. The idea was to set up wireless stations at each end of an armory and dispatch messages between them. Knowing that the company was short of operators, Sarnoff pleaded to be sent as assistant to an experienced man. Round and the others who knew about his studies and outside work put in a good word for him, and he was finally given permission to go.

The trip was another new experience—his first ride in a Pullman and his first taste of hotel living—but it proved to be much more valuable in a practical sense. The competence he displayed at the Louisville show was proof enough for the Marconi officials that he was well able to handle a key of his own. When he returned to New York, he was put in charge of the line connecting the main office with the Sea Gate Station, then the busiest point in the circuit. The long nights of study and practice had paid off. David was an operator. In time he became one of the fastest operators in the business, with a "fist," as it was known in the trade, capable of sending 45 words a minute, hour after hour.

Sarnoff not only worked for the Marconi Company, but he came to know Marconi himself, the already legendary figure of wireless, who had long been his hero. He had first seen the Italian scientist on a day when Marconi, on one of his trips to America, had called at the Marconi Company's office. The visit was a double piece of luck, so the story goes, because Marconi's visit came not only when David was in the office instead of delivering messages, but at the end of the day, when the scientist's departure coincided with his own. Fascinated by the mere presence of his hero, Sarnoff followed him through traffic to the Marconi Company's Front Street laboratory, where David himself would soon be working.

To many Americans, Marconi was still a somewhat unbelievable figure, a wizard who took lightning from the sky, as Franklin had done, and then made it perform for him. He had burst upon the American consciousness only a year after David had come to America. The papers had reported how the slim, intense Italian had stood on a hill in St. John's, Newfoundland, on a December day, 1901, flying a kite which carried his aerial, and from which he plucked wireless code signals from Poldhu, on the coast of Cornwall, transmitted on electrical waves in the atmosphere.

David had read about this incident, and indeed about every other aspect of the inventor's life that had appeared in print. He was overwhelmed when, as an employee of the company, he was introduced to Marconi, who took a liking to him at once. It may have begun as vanity on Marconi's part, a response to the obvious adoration of a young boy who dedicated himself to doing anything the inventor required when he came on a visit—running errands, begging to do chores, even delivering flowers to the ladies Marconi knew in New York. But then it became something more, and the two men were friends. The time was not distant when they could meet almost as equals, and when David Sarnoff had done more, perhaps, to utilize Marconi's discoveries for the benefit of the world than any other human being.

To David it was one of the most satisfying friendships he would ever experience. "I know what my association with Marconi meant to me when I was young," he once said. "I remember how patiently he explained to me the theory of the propagation of electromagnetic waves in space. 'David,' he said, 'we know *how* things work. We don't know *why* they work.' " That, to the young Sarnoff, was the fascinating part of the whole business—the search for the *why* of things, the ultimate truth. It became the search to which he dedicated his life.

As a full-fledged Marconi operator, Sarnoff now had the opportunity to get out of the office and serve wherever an operator was needed. Among his first assignments was on the steamship *New York* of the American Line, sailing from New York to Southampton; he was the only operator aboard.

As the ship moved out of New York harbor into the Atlantic, Sarnoff could not help thinking with wonder and gratitude of what opportunities the New World had already given him. It had been only nine years since he had first crossed the Atlantic, a poverty-stricken steerage passenger, with no visible prospects.

"So there I was," he has remarked, "nine years after arriving in this country, serving as the Marconi wireless operator on a first-class passenger liner, with a first-class cabin all to myself, with a uniform and gold braid, classified as a ship's officer, messing with the captain and the other officers, and entertaining and being entertained by the first-class passengers. No other country in the world, I thought, could have done such a thing for me."

At 17, Sarnoff was already a competent operator, but he wanted to know more, to do more, and when he heard that the Marconi Company needed an operator at its lonely Siasconset station, on the coast of Nantucket Island, he asked for the job. The Marconi officials hesitated. They were reluctant to send a boy so young and with so little experience to such a responsible position, but on the other hand it was difficult to induce an experienced operator to take this isolated post. Expediency won, and young David got the job.

"The principal reason I wanted the job was because of the fine technical library the company maintained there," Sarnoff admitted later. "My salary was $60 a month, certainly a modest sum, but I stood a watch only eight hours a day and was able to spend another eight hours studying."

After a few months on the island, Sarnoff could send and receive messages as rapidly and skillfully as any man on the coast, and he was rewarded for his proficiency by a raise to $70 a month. Of this he sent $40 home to his mother, and another $25 went for board at a nearby farmhouse.

His progress might have been satisfying to someone else, but Sarnoff was not satisfied. He had come to the island primarily to learn everything he could about wireless from the technical library at the station, and so he applied himself with his characteristic energy to that task. Before the first year of his two-year term came to an end, he had already mastered the station's books and

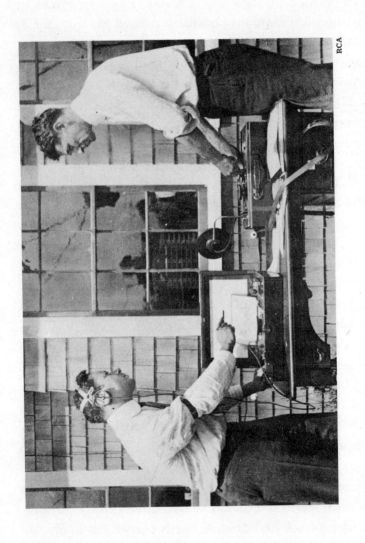

RCA

Sarnoff at the Siasconset, Mass., station, 1908

was eager to devour something else. The village of Nantucket, seven miles away, had a good library, and it was to this new store of knowledge that Sarnoff turned.

"I bought a secondhand bicycle cheap," he recalls, "and every couple of days I rode to town for a fresh supply of books. The island was a stormy place, and in winter the snow was piled so high and the winds were so severe that I could not use my bicycle. I used to walk to Nantucket and back frequently through blinding snowstorms. When the weather was too severe even for me to be out, I studied the company's technical books at the station until I knew them backward and forward."

Fresh from his Nantucket service in 1910, Sarnoff was ready for new experiences when he came back to New York, and the company provided them by sending him as wireless operator aboard such ships as the S. S. *Harvard*, operating between New York and Boston; and on several vessels of the Southern Pacific Line, sailing between New York and New Orleans.

These early training years were climaxed by the kind of adventure any teen-age boy, then or now, would have considered himself lucky to have. The Marconi Company was equipping several sealing vessels for voyages into the Arctic; and when it sent out a call for operators, there was no dearth of responses, in spite of the obvious perils. Sarnoff was one of those who volunteered, moved by his usual eagerness for new experiences. He was not deterred in the least by the talk he heard in the company offices about the dangers of the expedition, so formidable that some believed the men on the ships would never come back alive.

Assigned to one of the largest vessels, the *Beothic*, young Sarnoff at 19 sailed northward toward the Arctic ice pack and one of the most remarkable adventures of his life.

Chapter *4*

Arctic Adventure

On a frigid March day in 1911, Sarnoff came aboard the *Beothic* at St. John's to install and operate the ship's new wireless equipment for her sealing voyage to the Arctic. The vessel was owned by Job Brothers, merchants of that far northern port, who had ordered the new devices against the skeptical advice of other businessmen and most of the population, who could hardly bring themselves to believe in the invention.

None were more skeptical than the ship's crew, who watched with silent interest while Sarnoff strung up his aerial wires in temperatures of 20 degrees below zero—balmy, compared with what lay ahead for him.

"The crew of the boat was enormously impressed by the apparatus," Sarnoff remembered. "They were very suspicious of it, but since they were all anxious to

[69]

know how the rival ships were faring, they treated me with great courtesy. Most of the sailors were Newfoundlanders, an uneducated, illiterate lot who found it impossible to say 'Marconi' and compromised by calling me the 'Coni man.' The entire lot asked me daily, 'Any fresh news dis marnin', Coni man?'"

As the *Beothic* headed out of St. John's and began to thrust its prow northward toward the Arctic, she was accompanied by a sister ship, and the two of them butted the ice cakes together. It was the middle of March, but the water was still frozen solid. The two vessels traveled full speed ahead until resistance to the ice became too great for further progress. Then they reversed their engines, moved back a little, and crashed on through the clearing they had made.

The ships diverged at an agreed upon point, but the other vessel was no more than a thousand feet away when her captain signaled and shouted through his megaphone that the wireless had broken down. Only Sarnoff was qualified to repair it. The young operator regarded the ice sheet between the two ships without favor as he prepared to cross; and before he departed, he coaxed the ship's doctor into accompanying him.

"We were bundled up in heavy fur garments," he recalled later, "wore sealskin boots with spikes on the bottom to grip the ice, goggles over the eyes to prevent snow blindness, and carried gaffs or poles about six feet long to the end of which was attached an iron boathook to test the ice. Gingerly we made our way over to the other boat. It did not help matters that the crews looked on, laughing at our cautious steps. Finally, however, we reached our goal and after about six hours, the wireless was in working order again. We started on the return trip. It had grown late, there was a sharp wind blowing, and the cold was intense. To add to our discomfort, the ice was broken and huge patches of slob, or soft ice, were floating in the water.

"The only way to make distance was to jump from one pan of ice to another, disregarding the water between. The Newfoundlanders can jump on a piece of ice, no matter how small, and keep their weight on it just long enough to get to the next sheet. But unfortunately we were not Newfoundlanders. At every step of the way, we fell in the water, grabbing at the ice en route, which, after we had mounted it, promptly broke in half and gave us a thorough ducking. In a few minutes we were played out and lay gasping on an ice cake that held us for the time. The crew, which was watching our plight, yelled instructions to us and confused us more and more.

"Just at this crucial moment the captain of the boat set the bow of the vessel straight for us and ordered full speed ahead. I will never forget how I felt when I saw the big ship bearing straight down on us, smashing the very sheets of ice on which we stood. To be caught between the two heavy sheets of ice and jammed into jelly wasn't exactly my idea of the proper ending for an ambitious young telegraph operator. The captain, however, immediately realized his blunder and sent out a dozen or

[71]

more 'ice trotters,' as these expert sealers were called. The doctor and I were ignominiously handed from man to man, and as a crowning touch, the last man carried us on board."

As the ship plowed on northward, Sarnoff's initiation into the Arctic way of life progressed, with the help of the crew. Before long he could trot about the ice fields as though they were solid land. The skepticism about him and his apparatus had nearly disappeared, too, particularly when he was able to relay a message to the captain that his brother was the father of a son. He followed that with a message of congratulations from Job Brothers after he had reported by wireless the bagging of 2,400 sealskins in two days.

As he watched the men hunt the seals, extract their oil, and strip them of their pelts, Sarnoff became fascinated with the work, and with the seals themselves. He had brought along a camera and was anxious to take pictures of the animals.

On Sundays the boat stopped. The men rested and held religious services in the hold. No one was allowed to kill seals on that day; a curious mixture of superstition and religion made it an unpardonable sin to the sealers, a fact that nearly led to the wireless operator's demise.

One Sunday afternoon the crew was lounging on deck watching a devoted seal family playing on the ice below. A proud father seal was putting up his protective hood and making weird noises to amuse a baby seal and its mother, who were watching. The scene was too tempting for anyone with a camera. Sarnoff crawled over the side of the boat, camera in one hand and gaff in the other, and approached the little group stealthily.

He photographed the baby, but the father was still out of range. Sarnoff crept nearer to the young seal, thinking it might alarm the father enough to make him come out of the water and so bring him into the picture. Sarnoff came within five feet of the baby, but the father remained in the pool, his head above water, watching and motionless. The bold photographer came a little nearer, focused his camera on the big male, and deliberately took his picture. The click of the camera seemed to enrage the father. He pulled himself out of the water and waddled toward Sarnoff, throwing his huge bulk forward with surprising speed.

"I took to my heels and ran," Sarnoff says, "but as I ran, I had sufficient presence of mind to follow a zigzag course. This gave me a slight advantage because it was difficult for my pursuer to twist his big body at every turn. We had progressed only a few feet and the seal, with murder in his eye, was gaining on me. But the strongest man could not long hold out on the jagged, slippery ice; I was near exhaustion. My breath came in gasps, and my knees shook. Suddenly a shot rang clearly in the still Arctic air. While the crew had watched my plight with awful fascination, one of the sailors had dared to break the Sabbath law and shoot the seal. I think the captain believed privately that it would have been better if I had died a martyr to the law, but the man was never punished and all the men aboard heartily approved his action, none more heartily than I."

At his key in the wireless room, Sarnoff was meanwhile making friends, in the manner of operators, with men at other wireless stations who were at the far ends of his invisible lines. One of these was Jack Daw, chief operator at the lonely outpost of Belle Isle, the rocky, desolate island between Newfoundland and Labrador.

In an exchange of messages one day Sarnoff learned that Daw's assistant, W. F. Barrett, had fallen so ill that he could no longer take the relief trick. Sarnoff suggested that his friend, the *Beothic's* doctor, might be able to help. He had already prescribed by wireless for a seaman on a nearby vessel, and it would be no more difficult to radio medical advice across the 200 miles of ice and water that separated the ship from Belle Isle.

As the sealing went on, the doctor followed Barrett's case by radio, first with the curiosity that the use of the wireless still inspired in him, but then with professional interest and simple humanity as the story unfolded. Barrett's trouble had started with a simple toothache, which had developed into an abscess. Daw's medicine chest did not contain anything capable of dealing with it. Worse, Barrett's condition was soon beyond the reach of such uncomplicated measures, even if they had been available.

"Old man, I am up against it," Daw wirelessed. "Barrett seems to be getting worse instead of better. His cheeks are swollen frightfully, his temperature is alarmingly high, and he can eat nothing. He has been unable to leave his bed for a week. I have done all I could for the poor chap, but the suffering has nearly driven him mad and broken me up considerably. Our only neighbors are the head lighthouse keeper, a New-foundlander; his assistant and the assistant's wife—French Canadians. There are two lighthouse keepers on the other side of the island, but it is almost impossible to reach them as we are separated by ten miles of wind-swept ice. A Canadian Government vessel comes twice a year bringing fuel and provisions, but during the ice season we see no one. Only sealing ships can navigate through the ice, and it will be three months before the Government vessel arrives. Unless my assistant improves or secures prompt medical attention, I shall lose him."

That message came on a Sunday when, by custom, the ship stood still until midnight. When Sarnoff gave him the news, the doctor shook his head doubtfully. All he could do was to prescribe simple remedies, such as a diet of milk and hot water, and to request regular reports. As the days passed, Barrett's condition grew worse. His suffering was intense. Daw reported that the abscess was now so large that Barrett could scarcely open his mouth, and had to take his food through a tube. Sarnoff knew that drastic measures had to be taken if the man's life were to be saved.

"I summoned sufficient courage to place the serious situation at Belle Isle before Captain Barbour," he wrote later in the magazine *Wireless Age*. "It looked like a matter of life and death with poor old Barrett, for the last wireless reports stated that he was steadily sinking; and unless the abscess was given proper medical treatment, he could not hold out much longer.

"My efforts to have the ship turned toward Belle Isle were received with a kindly tolerance that held little encouragement. The ship was heavily laden and should it be taken into the ice floes, it might become jammed and remain for weeks with all the men and cargo on board. The captain explained what this would mean in financial loss and the danger to life and property in such an undertaking."

Dejected, Sarnoff went back to the wireless room and sat down before his instruments, trying to think of a way out. Through force of habit, he made the necessary adjustments that would put him in touch with Belle Isle. Jack Daw's insistent call pulled him back from his thoughts. The chief operator was anxious to know if anything had been done to get assistance for Barrett and pressed Sarnoff for details about the situation.

Daw's obvious deep concern for Barrett was so moving that Sarnoff could not bring himself to report how unpromising things were. Instead, he heard himself sending out exaggerated encouragement. Daw was so relieved by the prospect that the *Beothic* might come to his rescue that his touch on the key fairly snapped. Enthusiastic, hopeful messages buzzed into Sarnoff's earphones. He was sure everything would turn out all right. When was the *Beothic* coming? As soon as he knew, he would tell Barrett the good news.

"It was terrible!". Sarnoff wrote. "There I sat, staring the cold reality in the face, not one chance in a thousand that the captain would relent—and a man whose companion's life hung in the balance telling me across space how grateful he was to me for arranging his deliverance. Several times I started to interrupt and tell him the truth. But I could not bring myself to it. Then, when I had stood it as long as I could, I grasped at one despairing chance and broke in to tell him that everything was not yet settled, but it could all be fixed up if he would send a message addressed to the captain stating that his companion was suffering helplessly; that the end was near, and unless we hastened with medical assistance it would be too late.

"I delivered this message to the captain, enlisting the doctor's aid in placing the case before him. We made a lengthy and strong appeal that from all indications reached the captain's heart. But he would not say definitely whether he would attempt the journey. It was evident that our plea had a marked effect, but the question lay with whether he could or would bring the vessel near enough to Belle Isle to permit a landing."

Several days went by in choking suspense. Sarnoff went on sending encouraging reports, and the doctor continued to prescribe as best he could. Then came a report from Daw that brought an anxious frown to the doctor's face. Driven beyond his endurance by Barrett's

[77]

suffering, Daw had attempted to operate on his assistant with a hot knife, which, of course, had led to further complications and a threat of blood poisoning. In despair, Daw wirelessed that Barrett was dying, and the doctor himself carried this information to Captain Barbour.

The Captain heard the news stolidly, and still without a change of expression on his face, he disclosed that the vessel was headed toward Belle Isle and had been for several days. In fact, he said, it would arrive there in six or seven hours. "Maybe I didn't feel like hugging the old captain," Sarnoff said.

Preparing for the landing, Sarnoff and the doctor gathered up everything they could find which might represent comfort for the patient—blankets, pillows, fur robes, all manner of liquids, including those carried ostensibly for medicinal purposes. The crew, caught up in the spirit of the mercy mission, contributed from their own stores, specifying several pounds of tobacco for Jack Daw, whom they all admired for standing by his companion and trying to save him. By this time the crewmen were following the unfolding story with fascination, hanging on every wireless report that came over Sarnoff's instrument.

The *Beothic* stopped two miles from Belle Isle and a party of ten—the doctor, the captain's son, seven crew members, and Sarnoff—began the journey across the ice toward the wireless station and the lighthouse, which stood starkly against the horizon in the distance.

This was no mean expedition in itself. The Belle Isle station was situated nearly 500 feet above sea level on a mountain of ice and snow, which made it look like an insurmountable glacier. By the time the party reached the summit, only three members remained—the captain's son, the doctor, and Sarnoff. They were completely exhausted. The hardy crew members had dropped out along the way and returned to the ship.

Jack Daw and the lighthouse keeper, delighted with their appearance, were there to meet them, having followed the party's progress over the last portion of terrain. They conducted their welcome visitors to the little wireless station. There, on a rickety old cot in the coldest, dreariest room Sarnoff had ever seen, lay Barrett. His hair was matted and his hollow cheeks were covered with a stubble that made his pallor even more marked. He was emaciated almost beyond recognition after 20 days in bed that had wasted him away to a pain-wracked, undernourished shadow. He was, as Daw had reported, near death.

"When he saw us," Sarnoff reported, "he broke down completely and great gulping sobs shook his frame as the tears coursed down his cheeks. We all volunteered a few cheery words and the doctor took him in hand, quieting him so effectively that within a few minutes he was able to describe briefly his condition and answer questions.

"The doctor joined me a few minutes later and said that a very dangerous abscess had formed and three

RCA

At 19, when David was operator on the S.S. Beothic

of the teeth must be removed at once. While he was not a dentist himself, he was willing to undertake the operation with the instruments he had brought along; but he was rather reluctant about leaving the patient afterward without further aid in case blood poisoning set in.

"I laid the proposition before Barrett, telling him what was necessary to give him relief and mentioning the danger of blood poisoning to a man in his sorry condition. I told him he must take his choice—either submit to the operation then and there and take his chances, or, if he wished, we would carry him back to the ship and take him to St. John's.

"He made his decision without the slightest hesitation. Under no circumstances would he leave his colleague, Jack Daw. That man had shown supreme loyalty and consideration and given him untiring care and attention, and he would never desert him where there was any alternative. If it was to be, he would end his days there rather than leave his companion.

"So the operation was performed, and the available remedies administered. It was a complete success, I am glad to say, and even before we left he had been relieved of his suffering and was sleeping peacefully."

If there had been any lingering doubts on the *Beothic* about the value of wireless, this rescue dispelled them. The doctor was a hero on the ship, and as the fact that wireless had saved Barrett's life seeped into the consciousness of the crewmen, Sarnoff was almost equally so. Some of the Eskimos on the ship who had helped with the sealing were so overawed when they were told all the details of the story that they dropped on their knees before Sarnoff, much to his embarrassment, and murmured, "God bless you, Coni man."

There were two epilogues to the tale. The story spread rapidly and resulted in the creation of the Marine Medico Service, which has saved the lives of countless seamen the world over. Medical prescription by radio soon became part of the routine of ships' surgeons, and of the coast stations of the United States Public Health Service. It was, so to speak, Sarnoff's first unique contribution to wireless communications.

The second epilogue did not occur until April 1928, 17 years later, in the aftermath of one of the first attempts to fly the Atlantic, when the airplane *Bremen,* with its crew of three, landed on the Labrador coast. The first word of their safety, flashed to an anxious world, was signed by the wireless operator at Point Amour, W. F. Barrett. That name stirred memories in Sarnoff, who by this time was vice president and general manager of RCA. Twenty-four hours after Barrett's message had been received and printed in the newspapers, Sarnoff sent a message of his own flashing out from RCA's Broad Street station:

"Please telegraph me whether you are the same Barrett who worked with Jack Daw at Radio Station Belle Isle during 1911 when I was operator on seal fisher *Beothic* and visited you with doctor. David Sarnoff."

Several hours later the answer came back: "Greetings. Yes, am same dud. Hope you are having good time and health, and best fortune. Glad to hear from you. Thanks again for services rendered that 1911. Kindest regards. W. F. Barrett, Point Amour."

Nor was that the end of the coincidences. Further wireless reports from St. John's quoted Job Brothers as saying they had a fishing station on Greenley Island, where the fliers had landed, and that the men could be sure of plenty of food and comfortable quarters. Job Brothers, it appeared, were still in business. So, too, was Jack Daw whose name as operator appeared on further messages from the north, as the progress of the fliers was reported to the world. Daw was at one of these lonely outposts, still at his key, as was Barrett, who had been spared from death by the magic of wireless and 17 years later was able to use the same instrument to report the deliverance of three men who were blazing the trail for another era.

The Arctic adventure was over, and the *Beothic* was back in port. Sarnoff regarded the trip as an absorbing interlude in his continuing education in which he had learned much about seals and humanity; but he was eager now to continue learning—to take on bigger jobs and perhaps return to some kind of formal education in his field of a kind he could not get out of the company's library. He felt that his preliminary training was nearly over, and he was now ready for better things.

He was, in brief, ready to be Sarnoff, and he needed only a turn of events to send him skyrocketing on his way. That turn came as a result of one of the century's most spectacular events, and for young David Sarnoff it was just around the corner.

Chapter **5**

The Titanic Sinks:
A Career Begins

T he Marconi Company was well pleased with its operator, particularly with his stint on Nantucket, and they would have liked him to go back there, where good men were so hard to pin down for any length of time. But Sarnoff applied for a transfer to the Sea Gate station in Brooklyn, then the busiest wireless station in America. The company demurred. If he transferred he would have to take a $10 salary cut. Sarnoff agreed. His eyes were on the future. The transfer was made, and in a few months Sarnoff was made manager of the station, one of the most important such jobs in the system—and he was not yet 20.

From his vantage point in Brooklyn, Sarnoff looked around for new opportunities. One soon presented itself. John Wanamaker, the department store entrepreneur who was noted as a merchandising pioneer, had been examining the new invention, radio, with more than ordinary interest. He was always alert for anything which might advance his stores, and in radio he saw what he considered a dramatic possibility for advertising them. Consequently he had taken the revolutionary step of equipping both his New York and Philadelphia stores with powerful commercial wireless equipment.

The New York store needed an operator, and Sarnoff seized the opportunity. It was exactly the kind of job he wanted at the moment because the Wanamaker operator would be on duty only when the store was open, leaving the evenings free. That was what Sarnoff needed, because he had discovered simultaneously a way to get the technical education he wanted so badly.

Pratt Institute in Brooklyn was opening an evening engineering course for experienced men, which was designed to condense the usual three-year curriculum into one. Only a limited number of highly recommended students would be permitted to enroll. Sarnoff reasoned correctly that the Marconi Company would give him the necessary recommendation because anything he learned could only be to their advantage as long as he stayed with the organization. Thus in the fall of 1911 he began working at Wanamaker's and at the same time enrolled in Pratt.

It was a highly successful year scholastically. Of the fifty students who were permitted to begin the course, only a dozen survived by the end of the session, and Sarnoff's name was near the top of these. But before the academic year was over, the operator at Wanamaker's had a success of another kind which made his name known to the nation.

He was sitting quietly at his instruments on a dull April afternoon in 1912 when suddenly he heard signals in his earphones: *"Titanic* struck an iceberg. Sinking fast."* No details whatever, and no indication of the message's origin. Sarnoff immediately gave this information to the world through the press and concentrated on seeking further information through the air. In those days, the range of wireless communication was limited. To communicate with a ship as far away as 150 or 200 miles was regarded as a feat. However, Sarnoff kept pounding away with his key at the Wanamaker station in New York and alerted all ships at sea within range of his signals.

After several hours of straining at his receiver while an anxious world was waiting breathlessly for definite information, Sarnoff succeeded in establishing communication with the S.S. *Olympic,* which was then at sea some 1,400 miles from New York. The wireless operator on the *Olympic* told Sarnoff that the *Titanic* had sunk with a heavy loss of life; that the S.S. *Carpathia* had picked up many survivors and was bound for New York.

This was the first definite information received about the fate of the *Titanic,* and Sarnoff immediately gave it to a waiting world. Then he concentrated his efforts on establishing communication with the *Carpathia,* and kept asking for the names of survivors.

The implications of the tragedy raced through Sarnoff's mind as he bent over his instruments. Like all Americans who read the newspapers, he knew that the proud ocean liner *Titanic* had been regarded as unsinkable, and that she was already the ship of the rich and famous on their way across the Atlantic. She had sailed from Southampton on April 10, her passenger list crowded with well known names.

Her sinking, as it proved, was one of the most dramatic in the history of navigation, and is still an absorbing story a half-century later, as a recent best seller proved. When the disaster occurred, the news astounded the world and it was Sarnoff, sitting alone at his wireless receiver for 72 hours, who gave the world its only story of the tragedy.

As soon as the news had electrified the nation, President Taft ordered every other wireless station in the country to shut down, to eliminate every possible interference. Even so it took remarkable skill and endurance in those days of weak signals, primitive circuits, and deafening atmospheric interference to maintain contact with the sinking ship, and with those who were coming to the rescue of her survivors.

When word got around that a list of these survivors was being received by the Wanamaker operator, the store was besieged by relatives, friends, and the usual curiosity seekers. A police cordon was thrown around the building where Sarnoff sat, hour after hour, taking down the names as they were identified and transmitted. A few of the relatives were admitted to the wireless room. They included Vincent Astor, whose father was on the *Titanic*, and the sons of Isidor Straus and his wife, who were also on the ill-fated vessel. These anxious people came into Sarnoff's wireless cabin and watched over his shoulder as he received and wrote the names of the survivors.

"It was the most trying experience I ever had," he said later. "Imagine this pitiful crowd sobbing when the names of their relatives were omitted, or weeping for joy if the name of some dear one was announced."

The ship had been crowded with rich Americans returning from Europe. Vincent Astor sorrowfully learned that his father had drowned. The Straus family heard the tragic news that both Isidor Straus and his wife had gone down.

After his endurance trial, with the earphones never removed from his head for 72 hours, Sarnoff was given relief and hustled over to the Sea Gate station, where there was better communication with the *Carpathia*, which by that time was coming in with the survivors. Then, for ten hours more, he sat at the Sea Gate key, getting more names of the missing. When the last of the 706 survivors was identified, Sarnoff rose from the instrument, pale and shaking. He had a Turkish bath and a 12-hour sleep, after which he reported to work again, as good as new.

The repercussions of this tragedy were far-reaching. In the investigative clamor that followed, it was pointed out that a ship equipped with wireless was much nearer to the Titanic than the *Carpathia*, the chief rescue vessel, but her only operator was in bed. Obviously there must be better wireless service at sea, both the public and the newspapers cried. Congress, urged to act, soon passed a law requiring wireless equipment and operators on all oceangoing vessels carrying more than 50 passengers. The act also required an around-the-clock watch, with two operators, and an independent auxiliary source of power for the equipment. Within another year, more than 500 American ships were so equipped.

"Wireless" was a word on everybody's tongue in the aftermath of the tragedy, but oddly enough, its very usage doomed it as the common word for Marconi's invention. People began to saw off "radio" from its full name, "radio wireless telegraphy," and use it as a kind of shorthand. Within a decade it was part of the language. The United States Navy preferred the term radio-telegraphy, and adopted it, but in time "telegraphy" was shorn from that usage too.

The effect of the *Titanic*'s sinking on the fortunes of the Marconi Company was nothing less than spectacular. Every newspaper story—and there were thousands of them—about the tragedy and its aftermath constituted free advertising for the company, which was virtually certain to be mentioned in all of them. Wireless was suddenly in the public mind all over the world, and the astute Marconi managers took advantage of their situation. They found financiers more than willing to advance capital for expansion, and for buying up their chief competition, United Wireless Company.

Almost overnight the company's coastal stations increased from five to fifty. Another competing company was acquired and the number grew to 54. The Marconi Company was now the largest of its kind in the United States, a virtual monopoly, and its star was rising every day.

As for the gallant operator at the Wanamaker Station, his name was almost as prominent as the company's, and it was only natural that he should play a major part in the organization's sudden and rapid expansion. It was a tremendous undertaking, and Sarnoff, as the directors realized, was the one man in the company superlatively qualified to help them. He was made instructor of operator trainees, then inspector of all Marconi equipment being installed on passenger ships under the new laws, and the inspector of all stations as well. He rose rapidly from chief inspector to assistant traffic manager, assistant chief engineer, and then to commercial manager, under the benevolent supervision of Edward J. Nally, later the company's president, who understood what an asset he had in Sarnoff. Thus the young wireless operator, now a young executive, entered the infant radio industry on the ground floor, when it was having severe growing pains that he would do much to solve.

The beginning of World War I presented an immediate problem, because the Marconi Company was actually controlled from London, a point of irritation to the United States in the developing crisis. As soon as the American armies entered the war, the government seized most of the Marconi facilities for the duration—and found in Sarnoff a commercial manager who proved to be of inestimable help in harnessing those facilities to military uses.

War was of course the largest, but it was not the only problem the wireless industry faced. As in all major inventions, there was an immensely complicated patent fight to be settled. Westinghouse, General Electric, American Telephone & Telegraph, and the United Fruit Company were all in possession of basic radio patents, but the patents were so scattered that no one company had enough to make a complete transmitting or receiving system without infringing on the rights of one of the others. There were wild claims, counterclaims, and bitter courtroom battles. Lee de Forest himself had gone on trial in 1912, charged with selling fraudulent stock for his wireless system. The validity of this charge could be judged by its language, in which the invention that made de Forest famous was described as "a strange device like an incandescent lamp, which he called an Audion, and which device was proved to be worthless."

Nevertheless, so great was the ignorance of the judiciary as well as the public about what de Forest and his fellow scientists were doing, the inventor barely escaped going to jail and was given a stern lecture by the court on the advisability of "getting a common garden variety of job and sticking to it."

With the United States' entry into the war, government control brought a momentary stability to the industry, but as soon as peace came, chaos threatened once more. Only one man in Washington appeared seriously interested in doing something to avert a return to the disastrous prewar situation. Franklin D. Roosevelt, then Assistant Secretary of the Navy, made no secret of the fact that his division of the armed forces believed it had a large stake in the future of radio. Peacetime uses, as well as the role radio had played in the war at sea, had been convincing proof to him and to other Navy men that the orderly development of wireless transmission was indispensable.

The Navy, in fact, wanted government control of coastal and international radio in peacetime, and when Congress shuddered away from such a solution, some Navy officers then proposed to create a private American company controlling radio communications to and from the United States. This debate, in essence, was not unlike the controversy that broke out in the country early in the 1960's over control of a proposed satellite communications system. In the earlier battle, as in the later one, private enterprise was the victor.

As an executive of the Marconi Company, Sarnoff was in the midst of the struggle, but his thoughts for the moment were not directed primarily toward it. He was fascinated, as always, by the prospects and possibilities of the new medium, and wondering what could be done with it.

Sarnoff was well aware of the several interesting experiments that had already been made. As early as 1906, about the time young David was landing his first job with the Cable Company, an inventor named Reginald A. Fessenden, who had a station at Brant Rock, Massachusetts, was installing a high frequency alternator combined with a telephone mouthpiece and receiver. The alternator had been the invention of Dr. Ernest F. W. Alexanderson. Over this system, on Christmas Eve, Fessenden broadcast a recorded program that included a violin solo, a vocal solo, and a poetry reading. He followed these numbers with a request that anyone who had heard it report the circumstances to him at Brant Rock. He was showered with reports from ship operators at sea who told him how amazed and delighted they had been to get the broadcast, which was probably the first experimental radio broadcast ever made.

A year later de Forest began his experiments with radio broadcast talks and recorded music from his New York laboratory in the Parker Building, and in 1910 he scored a historic triumph by broadcasting Enrico Caruso's voice directly from the stage of the Metropolitan Opera during a regular performance. At least 50 listeners reported, with the same wonder and pleasure the ship operators had shown four years before, that they had heard Caruso's voice clearly.

With Dr. de Forest on the Audion's 40th anniversary

Sarnoff himself had performed a dramatic experiment of his own in 1914. That May he was on his way to New Orleans by ship as a delegate from the Marconi Company to a convention of Railway Telegraph superintendents. As he and a gathering of other delegates lounged about in the saloon of the steamship *Antilles,* 60 miles out of New York harbor, Sarnoff excused himself and slipped out to the radio room, where he put on the headphones and tuned in a shore station. Then he summoned his companions to come and listen. What they heard was a program of phonograph music coming from Sarnoff's old station at Wanamaker's, where he had for some time been directing experiments in transmitting music.

The delegates were astounded, and most of the voyage was taken up with endless discussion about the future of radio. It was the kind of discussion Sarnoff would be having all his life, and he enjoyed it thoroughly. He had no doubt about what was going to happen to radio, and he was glad to hear from the delegates that most agreed with him that at least it had wide possibilities.

Later in the year Sarnoff told a radio conference he would someday make voices and music from Great Britain audible in the United States, and there were still some skeptics in the audience who thought he was mad. Only six months afterward, in March 1915, he startled listeners to the Wanamaker station with a concert, unannounced, coming from the Savoy Hotel in London.

With all this impressive pioneering, however, radio could hardly have been called an industry in its pre-World War I stage. The general public knew little or nothing about it except what the *Titanic*'s sinking had inspired. Those who were informed about communications did not take too seriously de Forest's revolutionary invention of the three-element vacuum tube he called the Audion. With only a few exceptions, they could not visualize the Audion as it would shortly become—the heart of radio. In general, these experts thought of wireless, or radio, as an interesting toy, a comparatively unprofitable service that represented no real challenge to conventional telegraphy.

De Forest and the others had prepared the ground, but it was Sarnoff who in 1916 first proposed the bold and imaginative use of the new medium as a home instrument for mass consumption. For a young executive it was the kind of gamble almost certain to be coolly received by older if not wiser heads. At the time he was assistant traffic manager of the Marconi Company, an important but not an exalted position. But he sat down one day and wrote a memorandum to Nally, then vice president and general manager of the Marconi Company, a memo that has become famous in broadcasting history as the "Radio Music Box" memo. He wrote:

"I have in mind a plan of development which would make radio a 'household utility' in the same sense as the piano or phonograph. The idea is to bring music into the house by wireless.

"While this has been tried in the past by wires, it has been a failure because wires do not lend themselves to this scheme. With radio, however, it would seem to be entirely feasible. For example—a radio telephone transmitter having a range of say 25 to 50 miles can be installed at a fixed point where instrumental or vocal music or both are produced. The problem of transmitting music has already been solved in principle and therefore all the receivers attuned to the transmitting wave length should be capable of receiving such music. The receiver can be designed in the form of a simple 'Radio Music Box' and arranged for several different wave lengths, which should be changeable with the throwing of a single switch or pressing of a single button.

"The 'Radio Music Box' can be supplied with amplifying tubes and a loud speaking telephone, all of which can be neatly mounted in one box. The box can be placed on a table in the parlor or living room, the switch set accordingly and the transmitted music received. There should be no difficulty in receiving music perfectly when transmitted within a radius of 25 to 50 miles. Within such a radius there reside hundreds of thousands of families; and as all can simultaneously receive from a single transmitter, there would be no question of obtaining sufficiently loud signals to make the performance enjoyable. The power of the transmitter can be made 5 kw if necessary, to cover even a short radius of 25 to 50 miles; thereby giving extra loud signals in the home if desired. The use of head telephones would be obviated by this method. The development of a small loop antenna to go with each 'Radio Music Box' would likewise solve the antennae problem.

"The same principle can be extended to numerous other fields—as for example—receiving lectures at home which can be made perfectly audible; also events of national importance can be simultaneously announced and received. Baseball scores can be transmitted in the air by the use of one set installed at the Polo Grounds. The same would be true of other cities. This proposition would be especially interesting to farmers and others living in outlying districts removed from cities. By the purchase of a 'Radio Music Box' they could enjoy concerts, lectures, music, recitals, etc. which may be going on in the nearest city within their radius. While I have indicated a few of the most probable fields of usefulness for such a device, yet, there are numerous other fields to which the principle can be extended. . . ."

His idea was received with polite silence by the company. They valued their young assistant traffic manager, but apparently, as Sarnoff remarked without rancor years later, "they considered it a harebrained scheme."

There was some compensation for the cool reception his great idea had met. He was in love. Sarnoff had been far too busy with the development of wireless and his own career to think about girls until now, but his mother was about to do the thinking for him. After all, his mother said, David was 25 years old, and not getting any younger day by day, and still he wasn't married. It was time, she said, chatting with her neighbor in the modest Bronx neighborhood where the family had moved from the East Side.

The neighbor agreed. David was a nice boy, a good boy, she said, and he ought to get married. Her daughter, Lizette, was in a comparable position, and it was possible, it might be . . . . Both women agreed that these two likely matrimonial prospects should meet, and it did not take them long to arrange it.

Lizette and her mother were Parisian, or at least Lizette had been born there and the family had come to America from the City of Light. Somewhere her mother had learned English, more than well enough to conspire with Mrs. Sarnoff, but poor Lizette was still struggling with the new language and spoke not enough even to carry on a normal conversation. Sarnoff, needless to say, had never had an opportunity to learn French.

Nevertheless, under the watchful eyes of the mothers, they met one night when David paid a formal call. Years later Lizette recalled: "I made no impression on him, and he made none on me." The budding expert in communications could not communicate at all with the pretty Parisian, and both concluded that the evening had been a bore.

The mothers were dismayed, but hardly discouraged. The course of love, they agreed, never runs

smoothly; everybody knew that. They pushed and prod-
ded, gently and subtly, for the next four months. Lizette, meanwhile, perhaps sensing the inevitable, was
busy learning more English. When the two met again,
she could speak enough to rescue the evening from collapse. "This time it took," Lizette has said.

She did not have to make much conversation;
Sarnoff took care of that. But now she could understand
a good part of what he was saying and ask an intelligent
question once in awhile to stimulate him. Not that he
needed stimulation. He was full of the radio music box
idea and he poured out his dreams to this charming
young girl who listened so well.

"He tried to tell me of something that he was sure
would happen," Lizette later recalled. " 'We will have a
box,' he said, 'and we will push a button and out of it
will come the voice of Caruso.' He was so enthusiastic
that it was interesting just to watch him talk about that
wonderful, magical music box that was being born in
his head."

On July 4, 1917, they were married. The mothers
were happy, and the newlyweds were even happier, as
they are still today, nearly a half-century later.

In those days before the technological revolution
of the 1920's, the scientists were busy but Sarnoff's active, perceptive brain was often well ahead of them. Not
only did he visualize radio communications over long
distances, but he had begun to think in terms of shortwave radio at a time when the scientists were not yet well

[101]

RCA

Sarnoff as commercial manager of RCA, 1919

[102]

aware of its great possibilities. The engineers, in fact, thought him visionary; and Sarnoff knew they did not agree with him, nor share his beliefs, yet he was already displaying his tendency, later to become so well known, to hold out against all objections once he had become convinced an idea was feasible. His standard, polite reply to the skepticism of the engineers was a succinct, "I doubt whether a careful and exhaustive research has been made on this point."

The time was at hand, however, when he would have the power, the position, and the resources to prove his beliefs. In 1919, the Marconi Company began to negotiate with General Electric for exclusive rights to the Alexanderson alternator, at that time the best long-range radio transmitter available. Since Marconi was still controlled by British interests, the Navy was alarmed anew by what it considered a foreign threat to the independence of United States communications, and Assistant Secretary Roosevelt interposed the weight of his office. He sent emissaries to Owen D. Young, then vice-president of General Electric, in an attempt to persuade him that the Marconi move must be halted by creating an American super-company to control communications.

Young agreed, and in November 1919 the Radio Corporation of America was formed, with Young as chairman and the majority ownership residing with General Electric, although in the next two years both Westinghouse and American Telephone & Telegraph became large stockholders. The first act of the new corporation was to buy out the American operations of the Marconi Company.

Sarnoff was acquired, along with his company, and was at once appointed commercial manager of the new organization. He was, quite naturally, overjoyed by this development. For the first time in his life he found himself with an organization that was capable of doing anything it wanted to do in the field of communications. In his early years with Marconi, the company had been struggling, like Sarnoff himself, for a place in the sun. Then, when it suddenly found prosperity after the *Titanic* disaster, it was so busy installing marine communications that it had no time to break new ground before the war came. Now, with the war over and the restraining ties of absentee ownership broken, a new company backed up by ample capitalization was in a position to explore the future. It was all David Sarnoff could have asked for, and he wasted no time in grasping the opportunity.

Chapter 6

Radio Comes To America

Only two months after RCA was organized, Sarnoff was knocking on the door of its board chairman, Owen D. Young, with his "Radio Music Box" idea. In a new and longer memorandum, he repeated his original proposal and added a plan to connect the magazine *Wireless Age* with the sale of radio music boxes, "thereby making the Wireless Press a profitable venture."

Here was an example of Sarnoff's mind at work. In this plan he was not only proposing the manufacturing of home radio sets, then unknown, but suggesting magazine merchandising methods and forecasting editorial techniques that were still in the future. He wrote:

"Every purchaser of a 'Radio Music Box' would be encouraged to become a subscriber of the *Wireless Age* which would announce in its columns an advance monthly schedule of all lectures, recitals, etc. to be given in the various cities of the country. With this arrangement the owner of the 'Radio Music Box' can learn from the columns of the *Wireless Age* what is going on in the air at any given time and throw the 'Radio Music Box' switch to the point (wave length) corresponding with the music or lecture desired to be heard.

"If this plan is carried out the volume of paid advertising that can be obtained for the *Wireless Age* on the basis of such proposed increased circulation would in itself be a profitable venture. In other words the *Wireless Age* would perform the same mission as is now being performed by the various motion picture magazines which enjoy so wide a circulation.

"The manufacture of the 'Radio Music Box' including antenna, in large quantities, would make possible their sale at a moderate figure of perhaps $75.00 per outfit. The main revenue to be derived will be from the sale of 'Radio Music Boxes' which if manufactured in quantities of one hundred thousand or so could yield a handsome profit when sold at the price mentioned above. Secondary sources of revenue would be from the sale of transmitters and from increased advertising and circulation of the *Wireless Age*. The Company would have to undertake the arrangements, I am sure, for music recitals, lectures, etc. which arrangements can be satisfactorily worked out. It is not possible to estimate the total amount of business obtainable with this plan until it has been developed and actually tried out but there are about 15,000,000 families in the United States alone, and if only one million or 7% of the total families thought well of the idea it would, at the figure mentioned, mean a gross business of about $75,000,000 which should yield considerable revenue.

"Aside from the profit to be derived from this proposition the possibilities for advertising for the Company are tremendous; for its name would ultimately be brought into the household and wireless would receive national and universal attention."

Having forecast home radio, radio programs in magazines, a broadcasting system, and the future of RCA, Sarnoff sat back and waited to see what would happen. This time his superiors took him seriously. Two months later, E. W. Rice, Jr., then president of General Electric, asked him to estimate prospective radio business if his proposal were adopted, and Sarnoff responded with this uncannily prophetic letter:

"The 'Radio Music Box' proposition . . . requires considerable experimentation and development; but, having given the matter much thought, I feel confident in expressing the opinion that the problems involved can be met. With reasonable speed in design and development, a commercial product can be placed on the market within a year or so.

"Should this plan materialize it would seem reasonable to expect sales of one million (1,000,000) 'Radio Music Boxes' within a period of three years. Roughly estimating the selling price at $75 per set, $75,000,000

[107]

can be expected. This may be divided approximately as follows:

1st Yr.—100,000 Radio Music Boxes $ 7,500,000
2nd Yr.—300,000 Radio Music Boxes $22,500,000
3rd Yr.—600,000 Radio Music Boxes $45,000,000

Total ....$75,000,000."

The accuracy of this prediction was nearly total. In the first year RCA began making "Radio Music Boxes," 1922, its sales were $11,000,000, slightly higher than Sarnoff had figured, but the second-year sales were exactly what he had said they would be, and the third year was only $5,000,000 higher.

These figures resulted from a $2,000 initial investment, which was what the RCA board of directors allowed Sarnoff in 1920 after they had read and digested his two memos. With this pitifully small sum he was expected to develop a radio broadcast receiver and demonstrate its value. To anyone but Sarnoff it would have seemed hopelessly inadequate.

His cause was immeasurably aided only a few months after RCA placed its first production order with General Electric for Radio Music Boxes when a Westinghouse engineer, Dr. Frank Conrad, began the first broadcasts as they are known today over Station KDKA, in East Pittsburgh. To create an audience for these pioneer broadcasts, Westinghouse began to make and sell the crystal sets known to their lucky owners as "cat's whiskers." They were primitive, but they were good enough to permit people in Pittsburgh to hear KDKA. Then, in

November 1920, the station created a sensation by broad-casting the Harding-Cox Presidential election returns.

The response to that broadcast, and the shower of newspaper editorials and letters-to-the-editor that followed it, spurred on Sarnoff and everyone else at RCA, which had already begun to make crystal sets too, and early in 1921 followed them with the first battery-and-tube sets, known as Radiolas, which were made by General Electric.

It was a new Sarnoff experiment, however, that pushed the burgeoning radio business over the top and made it a national institution overnight. In the blistering early summer of 1921, the talk was not so much of the Harding "normalcy" the new President had brought to Washington as it was about the approaching heavy-weight championship fight between Jack Dempsey and the French champion, Georges Carpentier. Dempsey, a magnificent and colorful fighter, had caught the national fancy after winning the title from Jesse Willard in 1919, and it had been a splendid piece of matchmaking to pit him against the handsome and accomplished Carpentier, giving the fight an international flavor. With interest in the approaching battle at a fever pitch, Sarnoff concluded that this was the ideal event to put on the air. No other piece of programming could have attracted so much national interest.

Borrowing a portable Navy transmitter, he set to work arranging a remote broadcast from the ringside at Boyle's Thirty Acres, in Jersey City. Sarnoff enlisted the help of Major J. Andrew White, a popular figure himself who was then editor of *Wireless Age*, to help him in setting up the broadcast, and White in turn hired two radio experts to help him. After getting the permission of the Lackawanna Railroad to use its property, they strung an aerial from the clock tower on the railroad terminal in Jersey City to a steel tower. A galvanized iron shack, used by Pullman porters as a dressing room, was converted into a broadcasting station.

Tex Rickard, manager of the match, who was then coming into his own as one of the great promoters of the day, was quick to see the immense potential advantages of broadcasting to the fight business and arranged with the National Amateur Wireless Association to install receivers and loudspeakers in more than a hundred theatres, lodge halls, ballrooms, and barns from Maine to Florida, fairly well covering the eastern half of the country, which represented the listening range in those days.

When the gong rang for round one, Major White was at the ringside to give a blow-by-blow description, with Sarnoff at his side, and an engineer named J. C. Smith was in the galvanized iron shack to relay the description, which enabled between 200,000 and 300,000 people to follow the fight until Dempsey's victory by a knockout in the fourth round.

It was a triumph for radio. Not only was the fight heard by the owners of sets and those who had heard it in the public broadcasts arranged by Rickard, but it was listened to by many amateur operators whose reaction was most enthusiastic. It must have occurred to some of these listeners after the final gong that they had heard more details about the fight than were seen by a good many of the spectators who had trudged through the July heat and dust of a torrid afternoon to the oven of the wooden stadium. The possibilities of radio reception undoubtedly were unveiled to millions of people that day.

Most of these early listeners were using crystal detectors, which of course had no tubes. But the development of the vacuum tube as a sensitive detector and amplifier was progressing rapidly, and it proved to be the technical device that assured a quick expansion of the radio audience.

Another spur to expansion were the wireless amateurs, nearly 5,000 of them by that time, who had provided trained radio telegraphy operators for World War I and now were abandoning their dots-and-dashes to talk with each other through the radiophone. They were builders of receiving sets, and as they listened with them they constituted not only the beginnings of an audience but they provided a ready-made field testing laboratory for the engineers at RCA and other companies. The amateurs were the first to take up the vacuum tube and abandon the spark-gap crystal set. They were first to explore shortwave, and they were constantly helpful with the information they turned up in building their own transmitters and receiving sets. Many of them

[111]

graduated into the new radio industry as it developed into the giant it became.

That industry was virtually exploding in every direction. In the same year Sarnoff broadcast the Dempsey-Carpentier fight, he invited such world famous scientists as Albert Einstein, Irving Langmuir, and Charles Steinmetz, "the Wizard of GE," to inspect RCA's new transoceanic station at New Brunswick, New Jersey, where he gave them a demonstration. On April 29th of that year, he had been promoted to be general manager of the company.

A year later radio had become a national craze. Stations were springing up across the country like flowers after rain. Newspapers, not yet suspicious of the new medium as an advertising competitor, were helping to build the audience by printing do-it-yourself supplements for people who wanted to build their own sets. All over the country listeners were twisting the numerous dials of the new sets that were being developed, sitting up hour after hour with the headphones clamped to their ears until they took them off in the early morning hours, rubbing the circulation back into their numb appendages. Some of the amateur's symbols crept into the language. People told how they had sat up the night before getting "DX," meaning distance. Everyone listened to KDKA, but it became an indoor sport to log stations and a status symbol to be able to receive stations broadcasting from long distances away, the farther the better.

There was more for set owners to hear with every passing month. In the fall of 1922, the Princeton-Chicago football game became the first remote pickup of that sport transmitted for broadcast in another city, and it was only a few more years until the fans were listening to Graham MacNamee's breathless broadcasts from the Rose Bowl on New Year's Day. Music lovers heard the New York Philharmonic Orchestra for the first time on November 22nd of that year, and the regular Sunday concerts were soon a national institution.

A few months later the first radio commercial went on the air, and oddly enough it was for a product not often advertised by radio today—real estate. Sponsored by the Queensborough Corporation on behalf of its new apartments in Jackson Heights, the commercial introduced a gentleman from the firm named Blackwell who spoke for 15 minutes with considerable feeling on an extremely high level about Nathaniel Hawthorne and his ideal of the healthy country life (some listeners wondered if he hadn't confused Hawthorne with Thoreau) and how that life could be attained within sight of New York City by living in the rural atmosphere of Jackson Heights. The Queensborough Corporation paid slightly more than $100 for its message; the rate had been set at that figure for ten minutes of air time. Rates rose rapidly thereafter.

In the first two years of radio, between 1920 and 1922, Americans spent an incredible $100,000,000 for sets, tubes, headphones, and batteries. In another two years, the number of home receivers had reached an astonishing 3,000,000, most of whose owners in 1924 drew their chairs up close to the gooseneck speakers attached to the new superheterodyne sets so that they might better hear the throaty, fading voice of William Jennings Bryan, in the sunset of his career, speaking from the Democratic National Convention in Madison Square Garden. Broadcasting, Bryan proclaimed, was "a gift of Providence," and so it seemed to those who heard him.

Americans less than 40 years old today, to whom radio is an ever-present commonplace that travels with them anywhere they want to go, can scarcely realize what the new medium meant to those who were old enough to listen in the 1920's. A door to the world had opened for millions of people in small towns and on lonely farms. With a twist of the dial they were transported to Carnegie Hall, to distant football fields, to nightclubs and ballrooms where the new dance music was being played, and eventually to any place where a microphone and remote transmitting equipment could be placed, which meant that they were vicarious witnesses of news events. It was a transformation in national life perhaps even more remarkable than the one produced later by television.

Sarnoff seemed to be clairvoyant about radio's future as he pushed at its frontiers in a half-dozen directions. In a 1922 report to President Nally of RCA, he expressed again his confidence in the use of short, rather than long, waves and high-power stations as a means of attaining transmission speed and reducing static. He hounded RCA's executives to build super-power broadcasting stations until, in 1925, they constructed the first of many at Bound Brook, New Jersey, which was connected with the company's New York studios by three sets of land wires, linking ten stations. That hookup set the stage for the advent of network radio in 1926.

As early as 1922, Sarnoff had conceived the network that would become the National Broadcasting Company. In a letter of June 17, 1922, to E. W. Rice, Jr., honorary chairman of the board of General Electric, he had written:

". . . It seems to me that in seeking a solution to the broadcasting problem, we must recognize that the answer must be along national rather than local lines for the problem is distinctly a national one. . . . I think that the principal elements of broadcasting service are entertainment, information and education, with emphasis on the first feature—entertainment; although not underestimating the importance of the other two elements. . . . The service to be rendered distinctly calls for a specialized organization with a competent staff capable of meeting the necessities of the situation. Let us organize a separate and distinct company, to be known as the Public Service Broadcasting Company, or American Broadcasting Company, or some similar name."

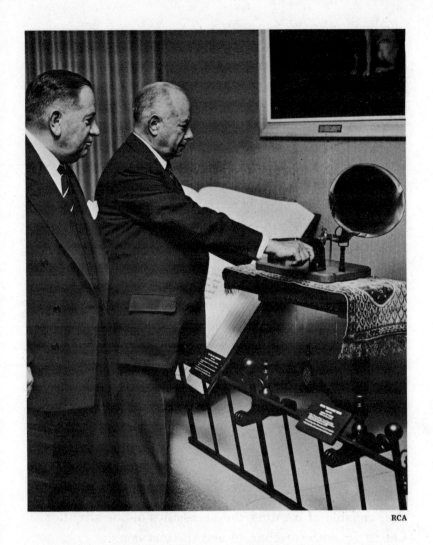

RCA

Sarnoff examines the first RCA-Victor phonograph

[116]

In 1926, the first step toward the realization of this idea was taken when RCA bought radio station WEAF in New York from the American Telephone and Telegraph Company for $1,000,000. RCA incorporated this property under the name of the National Broadcasting Company, and WEAF became the key station of what was known as the Red Network, as distinct from the later RCA-owned Blue Network, of which WJZ was the key station.

To those who were fearful that radio would do away with the phonograph (it was also freely predicted that it would mean the end of books and magazines), Sarnoff answered in 1922 that the opposite could be expected. All the industry had to do, he said, was to combine these two home instruments in one cabinet. Thus the radio-phonograph industry, a large part of RCA's product today, had its beginnings.

A year later Sarnoff was forecasting accurately that "everything which moves or floats will be equipped with a radio instrument; the airplane, the railroad, steamship, motorboat, automobile and other vehicles."

Everywhere he went RCA's general manager was a man who pointed the way toward the future. Addressing the New York Electrical Society in 1922, he demonstrated the possibilities of international broadcasting by calling England, France, Germany, and Norway with a telegraph key. He got a reply from each country.

Two years later, in 1924, he was standing in the auditorium of the University of Missouri before an audience of hundreds of rural residents who were there for "Farmers' Week." Picking up a long-distance telephone, he dazzled his listeners by sending a message via the RCA station in San Francisco to the Iwaki station in Japan, receiving an answer immediately over 14,000 miles of land and ocean. It was the first time radio communication had ever been established across an ocean, and then relayed successfully so far inland.

Sarnoff was fond of these demonstrations, which were always amazing to others, and sometimes even to Sarnoff himself. One day in the early 1920's he was talking by radio telephone to Captain Rind, of the steamship *America,* which was 800 miles at sea. During the conversation he was cut off, and as he would have in an ordinary domestic call, he jiggled the receiver impatiently and said to the operator when she answered, "You've cut me off."

"What number were you calling?" she responded, in a routine way.

"I was talking to a man on the Atlantic Ocean," Sarnoff said, beginning to enjoy the situation. There was a gasp at the other end of the line, but the operator was not one to depart easily from training. Her voice was frightened and subdued but she gave him the proper answer: "I will give you information, sir."

While he was talking with the *America,* his Irish maid at home (he had been making the call at a neighbor's house) happened to tune in the radio to Deal Beach, the station through which the call had been placed, and heard her employer's voice. She listened for an incredulous moment, then ran through the house to see if he had come home without her knowledge. Convinced that he was nowhere about, she fell to her knees, certain that Sarnoff had died somewhere and that she was in communication with his ghost.

"I got almost the same kind of shock myself not long afterward," Sarnoff said later. "I had made an address on the pallaphotophone, a device for photographing the voice, and the address had been recorded by the instrument itself. Two months afterward, at my home in Mount Vernon, I tuned in on WGY at Schenectady, 150 miles away, just in time to hear the announcer say, 'The next speaker will be David Sarnoff, who will talk about the pallaphotophone.' So there I sat in eerie silence, listening to myself lecture from 150 miles away."

In his ebullient and nearly always accurate prophesying, Sarnoff did not confine himself to radio. One of his most remarkable statements came in a memorandum dated April 5, 1923, which he submitted to the RCA directors. It read:

"I believe that television, which is the technical name for seeing instead of hearing by radio, will come to pass in due course. . . . It is not too much to expect that in the near future when news is telegraphed by radio—say to the United States, of important events in Europe, South America or the Orient, that a picture of the event will likewise be sent over by radio and both

[119]

arrive simultaneously. Thus it may well be expected that radio development will provide a situation whereby we will be able actually to see as well as read in New York, within an hour or so, the event taking place in London, Buenos Aires or Tokyo.

"I also believe that transmission and reception of motion pictures by radio will be worked out within the next decade. This would result in important events or interesting dramatic presentations being literally broadcast by radio through the use of appropriate transmitters and, thereafter, received in individual homes or auditoriums where the original scene will be re-enacted on a screen, with much the appearance of present day motion pictures.

"This re-enactment may, of course, be accompanied by music or speech of the original performance, thus conveying the impressions of sight and sound simultaneously to the broadcast listener and observer. The problem is technically similar to that of radio-telephony though of more complicated nature; but, within the range of technical achievement. Therefore, it may be that every broadcast receiver for home use in the future will also be equipped with a television adjunct by which the instrument will make it possible for those at home to see as well as hear what is going on at the broadcast station."

Less than four years later NBC's experimental television station, W2XBS, carried to a group of spectators in New York the voice and movements, on a tiny screen, of Secretary of Commerce Herbert Hoover as he sat at his desk in Washington. Television was still in the laboratory stage, but it was on its way.

Meanwhile, Sarnoff's restless, probing mind and apparently inexhaustible energies were carrying him forward both in perfecting and improving radio, and in advancing the fortunes of RCA. The company's chief drawback in these developmental days was that it had no manufacturing facilities of its own. It was primarily a sales agency for General Electric and Westinghouse. For the good of RCA, Sarnoff decided, that arrangement must be changed.

In 1929, Sarnoff successfully concluded one of the major deals of his life in buying the Victor Talking Machine Company, whose listening terrier, Nipper, and slogan, "His Master's Voice," was the best known trademark in the phonograph business. The experts were still skeptical about Sarnoff's contention that radios and phonographs were not natural competitors, but they changed their minds when RCA became the largest producer of records in the country, and eventually combined radio and phonograph in one home instrument, just as Sarnoff had predicted. The manufacturing and additional distribution facilities that were part of the Victor acquisition were also a part of Sarnoff's plan to acquire manufacturing strength.

Although the government antitrust action of 1932 forcing General Electric and Westinghouse out of RCA was a frightful blow, Sarnoff had built so well that he was able to pull the company out, in spite of the Depression and nearly $18,000,000 in debts resulting from the dissolution. He instituted severe economies, sold the company's control of RKO, and with these and other maneuvers contrived to get RCA into a position where it could take superior advantage of the new boom in network radio.

Good times or bad, Sarnoff had absolute faith in himself, his ideas, and his vision of the future. It was he who backed the work of Dr. Vladimir Zworykin, the Russian-born engineer who was responsible for the development of the all-electronic system for television that is the basis of the modern instrument. Sarnoff had known about Zworykin as early as 1923, when the engineer, then working for Westinghouse, applied for a patent on a device called the iconoscope, the retina of the television eye.

Six years later, when Zworykin was on RCA's payroll, he discussed the all-electronic system with Sarnoff, agreeing with him that this was where the future of television lay, rather than in the mechanical image-scanning systems used in television. Sarnoff told him to go ahead and work on the development of such an electronic system.

"He asked me how much money I needed," Zworykin recalled later. "I pulled a figure out of the air—$100,000. He said 'Okay.' Years later, when the general had spent $20,000,000 of RCA's money on television, and we were still experimenting away, he said he was just beginning to realize what a good salesman I was."

"I knew that $100,000 was only the price of admission," Sarnoff remarked not long ago.

It was characteristic of Sarnoff that in all his business maneuverings and preoccupation with scientific development, he did not lose his vision of what radio ought to be—a means of bringing culture and education to the ordinary citizen, as well as entertainment. Radio had its soap opera and its sports and its light entertainment, but it also had its cultural achievements, and most of them were instigated and encouraged by the president of RCA—as he became in 1930, at 39, succeeding General James G. Harbord, the retiring president of RCA who continued to serve as chairman of the board.

One of his early and striking successes in this direction came in 1928, when he established the weekly Music Appreciation Hour, under the direction of Dr. Walter Damrosch, the venerable conductor of the old New York Symphony, referred to lovingly by some of its members as "the barefoot Philharmonic."

All over America, on Fridays, schoolchildren gathered in classrooms and listened to the broad, cultured voice of Dr. Damrosch, unfortunately lending itself so easily to satire, saying, "Good morning, my dear young friends, and welcome to the Music Appreciation Hour." What followed, although it was sometimes derided by intellectuals, was an educational experiment of the utmost value and benefit. Children who had never heard a symphony orchestra play, and if they had would not have understood anything about the music they were hearing, now were led step by step to an appreciation of that music. Most of the young students who came to these classes unwillingly remained to listen with growing wonder as Dr. Damrosch unfolded the glories of the standard repertory. Older Americans, who grew up in small towns remote from any semblance of cultural activity, still remember these sessions with pleasure and appreciation for the new world opened to them.

Three years later Sarnoff satisfied a personal ambition when he arranged for NBC to broadcast directly from the stage of the Metropolitan Opera House on Saturday afternoons. After these first performances in 1931, the Met was a fixture on the NBC schedule for many years until it moved to another network.

Sarnoff's crowning achievement in bringing music to the millions was the creation in 1937 of the NBC Symphony Orchestra, an organization formed exclusively for radio, and for one conductor, Arturo Toscanini. The creation of this orchestra was a masterwork in itself. Armed with NBC money, the company scoured the country for the finest musicians available, and when the orchestra was completed, it represented a cross section of the best symphonic organizations in the nation who had given up some of their best musicians, attracted not alone by the excellent salaries but by the opportunity to play exclusively under the world's fore-most conductor.

Toscanini himself had been lured from retirement, after leaving the New York Philharmonic's podium, by the promise of a superb orchestra created especially for him. His contract provided that he could refuse to conduct if he did not like the orchestra. Naturally, there was some apprehension among Sarnoff and his associates, knowing the maestro's perfectionism, that their money and effort might be in vain.

When they walked up the gangplank to greet Toscanini upon his return from Italy, the maestro's first words were: "NBC Orchestra very good, first clarinetist not so good." Sarnoff and his aides were astonished until the maestro, with the gleam of sardonic humor he sometimes displayed, disclosed that he had been listening in Milan by shortwave to the preliminary concerts the orchestra had been giving before the arrival of its permanent conductor. The story is that Toscanini himself took the erring clarinetist in hand and personally coached him into being a first-class first-chair clarinet man.

That year, 1937, had been a milestone for Sarnoff. Not only had there been the creation of the orchestra, but he had persuaded the noted educator and former president of Yale University, Dr. James Rowland Angell, to become educational counselor for NBC. The subsequent experiments in education by radio that NBC made under Dr. Angell's direction laid a solid groundwork for much of what educational television is accomplishing today.

Then, early in 1937, Sarnoff had sat down at a desk in NBC's first television studio with Lenox R. Lohr, then president of the network, and Grover Whalen, president of the forthcoming New York World's Fair, and signed a contract committing RCA to participation in the 1939 Fair. He was already planning to make that participation the start of regular television service in the United States.

Before the fair opened, RCA's experimental television broadcasts had already produced some notable programs. Mobile television units had been developed as early as 1937, a year in which the studio staged about 130 demonstrations. Occasionally Sarnoff himself appeared in demonstrations, as he did in 1938 when the late John Golden, the noted Broadway producer, appeared with him before the cameras to discuss the new art and pronounced it as bringing "a new and glorious era in the world of the theater." That December, the NBC cameras were at the National Automobile Show in New York, and the promised era seemed, indeed, about to begin, as it did the following April, when the World's Fair telecast began with President Roosevelt's address, the first time a Chief Executive had been seen as well as heard on the air. Then, standing before a single camera and a pair of microphones, Sarnoff spoke. It was one of the proudest moments of his life, and a very long way indeed from Uzlian.

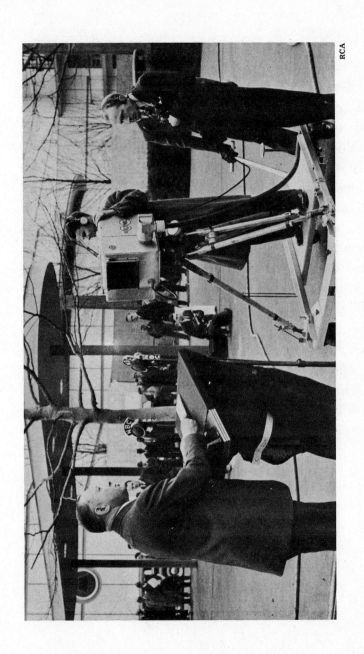

First commercial telecast, New York World's Fair

"On April 30th," he announced, "the National Broadcasting Company will begin the first regular public television program service in the history of our country; and television receiving sets will be in the hands of merchants in the New York area for public purchase. A new art and a new industry, which eventually will provide entertainment and information for millions, and new employment for large numbers of men and women, is here.

". . . And now we add radio sight to sound. It is with a feeling of humbleness that I come to this moment of announcing the birth in this country of a new art so important in its implications that it is bound to affect all society. It is an art which shines like a torch of hope in a troubled world. It is a creative force which we must learn to utilize for the benefit of all mankind."

The new era Sarnoff had been predicting for 17 years had begun.

Chapter 7

Sarnoff and Science

For a man who is not himself a scientist, David Sarnoff has been as close to the physical sciences as any human could be. He has built his career on them, a fact that has sometimes been obscured by his business genius; and if it were not for the many other facets of his personality, he could have spent his life in the laboratory, had he chosen.

His relation to science and scientists has been unique because he dwells in the scientific world without being actually a member of its community. He speaks the language, he understands the processes, but always his mind is a step beyond the laboratory in the realm of creative ideas that are not necessarily scientific. He could, for example, understand the scientific thought that went into the creation of television, but his mind

With George S. De Sousa, his first Marconi Co. boss

RCA

[130]

leaped at once to how it might be brought into the home, how color could be added, how color television could be transmitted around the world by satellite. He dreams the dreams, presents them to his engineers, and asks them to deliver. They have never failed him.

Long ago he established a practice of asking the engineers and scientists in the RCA laboratories to produce for him what might be, even to them, new and startling developments. Perhaps the best instance of these interacting elements at RCA is the story of Sarnoff's 45th anniversary dinner in the radio industry, an event that took place in 1951 at the laboratories in Princeton, New Jersey, which are named for him. In his speech that night, the General asked his assembled staff members to give him three gifts for his 50th anniversary, five years in the future.

He wanted, first, an electronic amplifier of light, to which he had already given a name—Magnalux. If the engineers could use amplifiers to magnify the intensity of sound waves, he observed, then they should be able to make an amplifier to intensify and create stronger light waves. For this invention he saw an immediate application in television, X-ray, and an almost limitless extension into other fields.

This, in itself was a splendid example of the Sarnoff mind at work as a unique bridge between science and industry, but he had two other gifts on his list. The second was a magnetic tape recorder for both black-and-white and color television, which would record

[131]

sound and pictures at the same time and replay them at will; and the third was an electronically air-conditioned room, employing a system without any moving parts.

When the 50th anniversary was held on September 30, 1956, at the Waldorf-Astoria Hotel, RCA's engineers had their gifts ready for the General. The true amplifier of light was presented first. It was a panel resembling a picture frame turned toward the audience and showing a portrait of the General himself. The light image falling from the projector on the reverse side was a thousand times less bright than the side of the panel turned toward the audience.

As Dr. Elmer W. Engstrom, then senior executive vice-president and now president of RCA, remarked to the guests, this gift had its immediate practical uses. For one thing, it would enhance the presentation of radar screens, providing bright pictures instead of the current dim images and also helping "as we move in the direction of seeing in near darkness."

The light amplifier had another use, Dr. Engstrom went on. It could be harnessed to the fluoroscope screens used by industrial radiologists, amplifying the image a hundred times, which meant that the subject and the radiologist would be exposed to a lower dosage of X-rays, and the radiologist could work in a lighted room instead of darkness. Further developments could make the light amplifier equally useful in medical X-rays, Dr. Engstrom added.

[132]

Sarnoff's second present from his engineers was the magnetic tape recorder for both black-and-white and color television. They had anticipated his birthday by making a public demonstration of this device two years before. At the time of the dinner it was still being tested in the NBC studios, but it shortly afterward became available to the industry and caused something of a revolution. Today the taped show is a commonplace and has had a profound effect on the whole structure of television broadcasting.

Having finished so far ahead of the deadline in the case of this particular gift, the engineers went on to produce something else with it: a prerecorded tape for use in the home—what the company calls a "hear-and-see" player. This instrument takes magnetic tape on which either phonograph records (or television programs) have been prerecorded and plays them back through a standard television set, so that people may see as well as hear the artist on the record. The logical next step, Dr. Engstrom noted, would be to develop the equipment so that it would record television programs off the air at home, so they could be seen again at will. Obviously the difficulties in putting these devices on the market are formidable, involving a jungle of legal complications as well as affecting other operations of the company, but the technique is ready.

Nor was that the end of the applications of this single invention. "A further development," Dr. Engstrom went on, "is to have a simple . . . camera so that we can by electronic photography make records of our friends and our family and immediately play these back on such a player through our television receiver."

In producing the General's third gift, the electronic air conditioner, RCA's engineers came in through the back door, so to speak, and invented first an electronic refrigerator without moving parts, and consequently noiseless, with a cooling compartment for food and a freezing compartment for ice cubes. The electronically air-conditioned room, which was demonstrated next day at Princeton to the General and the press, again employed no moving parts. The cooling, accomplished by wall panels, was essentially draft-free, a highly desirable situation in air conditioning.

Responding to the presentation of these wonders, the General remarked amiably: "A few of the scientists and research men who heard me make these specific challenges to their ingenuity wondered if I quite grasped the toughness of the problems involved. If I did, they said, I might not have had the gall to set a five-year time limit for their solution. But I have often had more faith in these men than they had in themselves. I had no doubts that they could solve these problems, and I even thanked them in advance for the presents I confidently expected to receive tonight. Of course I realize that in part they are still in what engineers call the developmental stage. But the fact remains that in five short years they have succeeded in turning what were bold dreams and hopes into proud realities."

[134]

Visiting RCA's Rocky Point station with Marconi

Sarnoff, in these words, aptly summed up his relationship to science and scientists for the past half-century. He has been the friend of many of them, and as he says, the greatest were "plain, humble, friendly men."

"My chief impression of Marconi was always of democracy," he once recalled. "I remember one day an Italian boy came in to shine his shoes. Marconi got interested in something the boy said and detained him for half an hour, talking to him eagerly in Italian and shaking hands when they parted.

"The greater the scientist is the humbler seems to be his attitude. If you asked Steinmetz, 'What is ether?' he told you that he wished he knew. A college sophomore, on the other hand, would answer glibly that ether is a medium through which electric waves travel."

When Steinmetz, Langmuir, and Einstein were being shown the new radio station at New Brunswick in 1922, Sarnoff remarked that Einstein, instead of making new prophecies about radio, seemed almost awed by the magnitude of the concrete development of theories that he understood perhaps better than any of the others. He lived in the realm of theory; to see the theory realized impressed him nearly as much as it would a layman.

At the 1922 affair, Einstein, Steinmetz, and Langmuir rode out to New Brunswick together in an automobile and, according to Sarnoff, "they carried on an astonishing conversation in three languages—German,

French, and English. A rapid fire of ideas went back and forth, and the three promulgated theories and problems enough to keep the rest of the scientific world busy for a generation. They discussed the internal structure of atoms and the inmost secrets of science in much the same manner that we ordinary mortals would debate what to have for dinner."

Sarnoff was also a friend of John Hays Hammond, Jr., the inventor and electrical engineer who eventually became a director of RCA. "When he gave his first demonstration before officials of the Marconi Company," Sarnoff says, "I remember that the tall young fellow carried all his equipment in a black box and each part was painted black. This was a camouflage arrangement to make sure that nobody would pirate his idea. Hammond was a latter-day descendant of a long line of gentlemen scientists, men of means who might have been content to live without work, but who have wanted to invent for the joy of it. Cavendish and Faraday were among this group; and so was the Marquis of Worcester, who built one of the original steam engines."

One of Sarnoff's favorite stories about Marconi concerns the time the two men were cruising and experimenting on board the inventor's yacht, the *Electra*. "We were experimenting with shortwaves, endeavoring to establish communication with Australia from the English Channel. It was five o'clock in the morning when we finished our experiments for the day. We were about

RCA

Celebrating 35 years of transatlantic transmission

to retire when he said to me: 'David, there is one thing I would like to know before I die—I know *how* this thing works, but I would like to know *why.*' Like many before him he died without an answer to his question."

Sarnoff himself has at least two inventions to his credit, both of them RCA patents. On December 7, 1948, the Patent Office gave him a patent for a secret signaling system; and on October 16, 1951, his second patent was issued, this time for what he called an "Early Warning Relay System," combining the principles of television, radar, and microwave relay, and intended to be applied to "guided missiles and air combat."

At RCA, the General has been the moving figure behind most of the company's remarkable more recent products. He was responsible for the development of the world's most powerful radio station, a 1,200,000-watt transmitter at Jim Creek Valley, in the State of Washington, built for the Navy. In 1953 Sarnoff tapped out the first message to be sent from this awesome installation—a message from Admiral Robert B. Carney, then Chief of Naval Operations, which was received by every Navy ship and outpost around the world.

A year later Sarnoff demonstrated the direct conversion of nuclear energy into electricity by telegraphing a message using power derived from RCA's experimental atomic battery. In that same year he saw the concept of military television he had envisioned 20 years before put to a practical test in a demonstration at Fort Meade, Maryland, where General Matthew B. Ridgway, then

Army Chief of Staff, used a combat-type Vidicon camera RCA had developed for armed forces use.

One of the devices that earned him the accolade of "imaginative cold war strategist" was a hand-operated phonograph capable of delivering three-minute messages, to be used behind the Iron and Bamboo curtains. This was only one of several devices developed by RCA as a result of Sarnoff's marshaling of the company's technical resources several years ago to help the United States government in its propaganda war against Communist countries.

Since radio was the General's first love, his pride in RCA's part in developing the transistor set is understandable. "The master key to the continuing expansion of electronics," he has called it. Sometimes, regarding one of the improved models that the company is constantly turning out, Sarnoff cannot help marveling at how far science has come since the days when he sat at a bench in the lonely Siasconset station on Nantucket, tapping out messages through his wireless key.

Inevitably in conversations about science, the old argument comes up about the supposed conflict between scientific thought and religion. Sarnoff heard that argument as a boy, as boys hear it today, when the faith in which they have been brought up is challenged by the cold, material facts of science. As one who has lived all his life with science and yet retains a strong religious belief, the General's views on this subject are worth hearing.

[140]

"The claim that there is an inherent conflict between science and our immortal souls—that science is the natural enemy of the soul—does not stand up under examination," he said. "The man in an airplane is not necessarily less devoted to truth, justice, and charity than his forefathers in oxcarts. Virtue does not necessarily go with primitive plumbing, and human dignity can be nurtured in a skyscraper no less than in a log cabin.

"Science begets humility. Its every discovery reveals more clearly the divine design in nature, the remarkable harmony in all things, from the infinitesimal to the infinite."

Religion and science are not antagonistic in any sense, the General often remarks, when the conversation turns to spiritual values in relation to proved scientific fact. They are, instead, partners in the constant effort of man to learn more about the universe he lives in. They represent two potent but compatible forces, and Sarnoff is convinced that it is only through their union that a world of peace and brotherhood can be achieved.

"But the mortar of brotherhood is not a product of the laboratory," he warns. "It must come from the human heart and mind, and therein lies the crux of man's dilemma. He has not yet learned, as a social and economic creature, to keep step with his science. He is technologically mature, and a spiritual adolescent. Having conquered nature, he must now learn to conquer himself.

"The devices which science has given us are neither good nor evil in themselves. Their capacity for good or evil lies in the use we make of them. Thus, not in the laboratory, but in the human heart, in the realm of the spirit, lies the challenge of the future."

In his view of science and religion, Sarnoff follows the beliefs and ideas of many scientists, particularly the astronomers, who see in the grand design of the universe and the interrelationship of everything in it, the evidence of an infinite Power beyond human comprehension or understanding. In man's efforts to discover the secrets of his own body, of the earth he inhabits, and of the limitless space around him, he is only unfolding, these scientists say, a pitiful few of the details in the Master Plan that makes the universe a cosmic whole, not a haphazard collection of stars and other fragments of matter floating in a cosmos created by accident.

Viewed in this light, the achievements of the greatest scientists are seen in their proper perspective, the General believes. It is enough to make the most brilliant man humble.

Chapter 8

In The Public Service

Οne of the lessons a man learns when he is in the public eye is that his time is not entirely his own. Government calls on his services in wartime and peacetime. Education has its own demands. Most men of eminence in the nation are called upon frequently to offer their knowledge and experience where it can be most useful, and few refuse. Nor is it a oneway transaction. They, too, learn from their service.

Much of David Sarnoff's public service has been involved with the armed forces, dating to World War I, when President Wilson called upon him and the Marconi Company to help equip the American forces with wireless. It was a monumental task, which had to be accomplished in an incredibly short period. Perhaps no other man, certainly no other company at the time, could have done it.

The Army recognized his services in 1924 by appointing him a lieutenant-colonel in the reserves of the Signal Corps on December 11. It was typical of Sarnoff that he did not rest on his commission as a civilian. He meant it to be no empty title, and consequently went down to Washington in 1927, where he completed a course of study at the War College. Four years later, he was promoted to the rank of colonel.

Meanwhile, having done his part to help win that first great conflict, he was called upon to participate in the unsatisfactory business of cleaning up after it. In 1929 he left New York for Paris on the steamship *Aquitania,* as an assistant to his old boss, Owen D. Young, who had been made chairman of the United States Reparations Commission. Other members of the commission included J. P. Morgan, Thomas Lamont, and Nelson Perkins, all internationally famous financiers.

It was one of the three memorable trips Sarnoff has made during the course of his career, as he is fond of recalling. The first was his trip to America as an immigrant boy, and the second his 1908 voyage as a wireless operator on the S. S. *New York,* traveling first class on a route he had traversed by steerage only a few years before. Now, in 1929, he was a member of an important commission appointed by President Hoover to reach final agreement with the Germans on the debts and other problems still unresolved more than a decade after the close of the war. Their task, too, was to replace the Dawes Plan with what later became the Young

Plan, both schemes to put the German reparations problem on some sound and sensible basis.

As Young's assistant, Sarnoff's particular task was to negotiate on behalf of the Allies with the formidable Dr. Hjalmar Schacht, the financial wizard of the German Republic, who represented his country, even then on its way toward a second attempt at conquering the world. The mission was foredoomed to failure, but Sarnoff and the other financial and industrial giants on the commission had no way of knowing it. They negotiated in good faith. Sarnoff's own negotiations with Schacht went on for six weeks, at the end of which he believed that the pressing problems of the time had been solved. So they might have been if the agreement that was signed in Paris had been honored; it was, instead, repudiated by Adolf Hitler, along with the hopes of mankind that it represented.

"The impressive and human part of that trip to me," Sarnoff recalled later "was not only the companionship of these important men, who were much older and wiser than I, but the fact that I was a member of that group, and that we were met at Cherbourg by high officials of the French Government. This time, no passport problems, no baggage problems, no customs problems. Our reception was conducted with the pomp and protocol that the French are so expert in providing. We were taken from a special tender to a private train supplied by the French Government, which whisked us to Paris and the comforts of the Ritz Hotel.

[145]

"I shall never forget the moment, during this third trip, when I stood on the deck of that tender, reflecting upon this novel experience. The picture that flashed through my mind then, as it had in 1908, was my first crossing of the Atlantic in the steerage. I thought of the contrast between the two trips and the fact that this could happen only in America. . . . I remember saying to myself, 'God bless America.'"

Sarnoff, of course, could not assess his own work in Paris, but Owen Young later wrote of him: "He was our principal point of contact with the German delegation, and he did an extraordinary piece of work in negotiating for us with them. . . . One could easily see that each man in the group of American delegates and experts was effective and at one time did a job that saved that conference; each seemed to have a part in the crisis which prevented it from being wrecked, and that can be said of Sarnoff in particular, for there came a time when only one man could save the situation, and that arose toward the end with Sarnoff and the German delegation." Sarnoff did the necessary saving.

When World War II came, wrecking the hopes alike of the commission and mankind, Sarnoff not only threw the immense resources of RCA behind the war effort, but also put on his uniform. After a short time in the office of the Chief Signal Officer in Washington, he was assigned overseas, where he served as Special Consultant on Communications to General of the Army Dwight D. Eisenhower, at Supreme Headquarters. There he was nominated for promotion to Brigadier General in November 1944, a rank that the Senate approved on December 6.

If his grandchildren ask him what he did in the great war, the General can show them the letter General Eisenhower wrote to him when both men were still at SHAEF. It read:

"Your contribution in anticipating and preparing proper communication facilities for the Press prior to D-Day and immediately thereafter was notable, and your initiative in reopening Radio Paris deserves commendation.

"You have, as Acting Chief, Communications Section with the United States Group-Control Council, placed the benefit of your years of experience in the field of world-wide communications at its service, and this guidance will undoubtedly contribute to the Council's future success.

"I wish to express my sincere appreciation at this time for the services that you have rendered to your country and to this headquarters."

Two Presidents followed General Eisenhower in honoring Sarnoff for his services. President Roosevelt awarded him the Legion of Merit in October 1944, and in February 1946, President Harry S. Truman presented him with the Medal of Merit for services "of inestimable value to the war effort." The citation went on to commend him for placing "the full resources of his company at the disposal of the Army whenever needed,

Planning for D Day with one of Eisenhower's staff

*Congratulations on reaching rank of general
from General H. C. Ingles,
Chief Signal Officer, U. S. Army*

[149]

regardless of the additional burden imposed upon his organization. He encouraged key personnel to enter the service, and at his direction RCA engineers and technicians rendered special assistance on numerous complex communications problems. He fostered electronic advances which were adapted to military needs with highly beneficial results. . . ."

While he was in Europe, the General's astonishing brain was, as usual, leaping beyond the problems with which he had to deal at the moment. He has never been a man to confine his planning to one thing at a time. Thinking about how America might better make her voice heard abroad, he conceived the idea of a radio program that later became the Voice of America. President Roosevelt was told of the idea, but it seemed better suited to him as a postwar propaganda device. Sarnoff uses the word "propaganda" in its best sense. As one of the Voice's most ardent advocates, he believes that it is one of the ways by which better communication between men can take place, and that has been the purpose of his life.

Whenever the government has turned to Sarnoff for help, his response has always been extraordinary, and never more than in 1955, when the military reserve program appeared to be faltering, and President Eisenhower named the General as chairman of the National Security Training Commission in an effort to get the program moving again. The promotion drive Sarnoff organized was a model of its kind, in which the entire resources of the National Broadcasting Company were used in the most lavish and imaginative way possible. More than 6,000 radio and television programs, worth nearly $2,000,000 in air time, were employed to boost the reserve program. Television's brightest stars—such entertainers as Dinah Shore, Perry Como, Garry Moore, Phil Silvers, Martha Raye, and Ed Sullivan—became "recruiting officers." The nation was made reserve-conscious overnight, and enlistments showed a phenomenal increase. When the drive was over and the Defense Department had pronounced it a complete success, Sarnoff, an advocate of economy in government, turned back to Congress $12,000 of the $50,000 it had appropriated for his work.

The General is constantly thinking up new ways to fight Communism. In April 1955, he submitted a memorandum to President Eisenhower urging the government to adopt a bold "Program For A Political Offensive Against World Communism" that he had devised. It soon became one of the most widely reprinted and discussed plans in the cold war, appearing as required reading in numerous college courses and in military officer training programs. This and other statements he has made in support of his belief that "the best way to prevent a hot war is to win the cold war" have made him one of the private citizens most often quoted on the floor of the Senate and House.

Sarnoff has enough medals and citations for a dozen men; only a few of them have been mentioned here.

Reviewing Merchant Marine Academy midshipmen

One of those he treasures most is a citation from the United Nations, presented to him in 1949, by Trygve Lie, then secretary-general. It was given for his "notable cooperation in the development of public understanding of the work of the United Nations, and for his contribution in the field of human rights through the advocacy of concepts of freedom to listen and freedom to look as fundamental expressions of freedom of information."

That honor, and one other, he counts among the highest. In August 1961, members of the Senate invited him to Washington for a luncheon on Capitol Hill. As the New York *Times* remarked, "Several Senators present said they could not recall an occasion on which so many legislators had come together to honor a private citizen." There were 32 of them, and Vice-President Lyndon Johnson in the bargain.

The citation given to him that day read: "In commemoration of his dedicated service and outstanding contributions to the advancement of communications and electronics in the United States of America." It was signed by all those present.

Out of all these honors, public and private, and as the distillation of his more than half a century in communications, the boy from Uzlian has learned a great deal to be passed on to the boys from every quarter of the globe who are now coming after him—the Sarnoffs of tomorrow. The General likes to talk about young people, and not in the sententious tones of the old man giving advice to another generation. He is deeply interested in youth and its problems because they belong to the future, and it is the future that has always fascinated him.

"The most important factor to keep in mind is to continue your education," he likes to urge youngsters who come to him for advice. "Science and industry will reward you for your talents and energy. Out of your efforts may come new inventions, new products, new processes and services. There is everything yet to be accomplished in our lives and in our work. What man has done, man can do better.

"Accept the fact that the only certainty in your lives will be change—and you will be in a better position to assimilate it without mental indigestion and moral confusion."

The General is concerned because so many young men today seem to be preoccupied with security. "Some young people," he says, "have adopted Ferdinand the Bull, smelling flowers from dawn to dusk, as the symbol of the good life. I have been disappointed, at times, to find boys in their twenties, or even in their teens, worrying about pensions and old age security when they will have reached sixty-five. There seems to me something unhealthy where youth is so lacking in confidence. Maybe we have to re-learn the meaning of ambition and of struggle. When has anything worthwhile been attained except by overcoming obstacles? And the thrill, believe me, is as much in the battle as in the victory."

In his vigorous 70's himself, in spite of recent serious operations, Sarnoff has no patience with retirement, for himself or anyone else, although he recognizes it is not the same for every man. "It depends on what he is doing and what he has to offer." A man who retires because he is tired of his job is headed for misery, Sarnoff believes. "If he could retire from himself, that would be fine." His advice is: "Change—don't retire. Find another place where you can express yourself. To retire to self-indulgence doesn't mean anything."

The General has further sound advice to offer young men. He notes how curious it is that problems, crises, and conflicts that seem the most distressing when they are happening are among the most satisfying of memories when they enjoy the perspective of time. "I offer this consolation in passing," he says, "by way of consolation to young men and women wrestling with tough problems today."

As for careers, says this man whose own career has been so remarkable, state of mind is a highly important factor. It is quite possible, he thinks, for a man to condition his mind so that it either enables or prevents him from going forward and doing things. "You can poison your own mind and limit your own capacity. Don't admire the fellow who says he has an open mind —it is usually a mind with nothing in it. A man who has a state of mind based on knowledge and wisdom, experience and reason, has won half the battle. State of mind based on balanced judgment is a precious possession, but being unreasonably optimistic means nothing to me, nor does being excessively worried."

His career advice, Sarnoff says, could be summed up in four simple rules, which he has followed through his own life:

1. Work and live in such a manner that you will be able to serve others.

2. Plan, so that you will be able to advance something.

3. Achieve, so that you will leave the world a little better than you found it.

4. Find as much peace of mind as you possibly can, for that is happiness.

Again and again in his speeches to young people, the General emphasizes the importance of education, particularly in science. America, he thinks, is still a nation of scientific illiterates whose great achievements have been the work of a relatively few men. There is need for a great outpouring of young scientists to meet the challenges of today.

"To me," says Sarnoff, "it has always been a curious fact that we, as a people, do not regard science as a part of education. No man can be considered educated, in the sense that this age must think of education, if he does not know why an airplane flies, or how his telephone works, or what happens when he turns his radio on.

"Science is changing the world, and most Americans neither know nor care how these changes are being brought about. Today every officer of government, every lawmaker, is confronted with all sorts of scientific and technical developments which affect the political, economic and social problems that are a government's main concern. A businessman, no matter what his field, is confronted every day with technical and scientific breakthroughs that may threaten him with disaster—or hold out the promise of great achievement. Yet lawmakers and businessmen alike must turn for advice to technical people whose language they may not even understand."

To bring up a new generation of scientifically literate Americans, the General believes, it will be necessary to begin with children at an early age and expose them to the drama of scientific exploration. He is an advocate of bringing the best scientists out of their research laboratories from time to time to teach and inspire young students, who will make the great discoveries of the future.

As usual with his beliefs, Sarnoff has a plan to make this dream a reality, and at RCA he has set an example that he hopes others will follow. For some time now scientists from the company's various laboratories have been appearing at junior and senior high schools in New York City, in a series of lectures and seminars. These sessions are fitted into the regular curriculum, so that it will not be disrupted, but the idea is to stimulate the students' intellectual curiosity, to push their minds beyond the textbooks to the edge of the unknown. That, as the General well knows, is where there is excitement and challenge.

Sarnoff emphasizes how easy it would be to carry out his idea everywhere in the country, since more than 60 per cent of American scientists work for industry or government in laboratories and workshops well distributed over the states, nearly always close by to school systems where often their own children go to school. Ironically, in many of these same schools students cannot get a scientific education because there is a shortage of trained teachers.

Sarnoff first made his proposal for an industry-science teaching program in January 1956, when he was being presented with the Forrestal Memorial Award in Washington. He suggested that the program be tested on a five-year basis at the high-school level. Characteristically, he kept plugging away at it, reiterating the plan three months later before the Subcommittee on Research and Development of the Joint Congressional Committee on Atomic Energy, and again in January 1958, before the Preparedness Investigating Subcommittee of the Senate Armed Services Committee.

To those who were skeptical of the time and administrative effort it would take to implement the program, Sarnoff said simply: "The beginnings of great strides in progress often have been found in tiny seeds. The steam engine was born in a tea kettle. The airplane came out of a bicycle shop. The first automobile sputtered and moved in a carriage shop. Broadcasting started with an amateur station in a private garage. Today the architects of the future must be sought among the young people in the schools of America. It is of vital interest to the nation that their vision be stimulated, and that paths be opened to them for its realization."

When no action was taken on his plan, Sarnoff proposed it all over again in January 1962, in an article in *This Week* magazine. Then he presented it personally to Mrs. Anna Rosenberg, former assistant Secretary of Defense, later a member of the New York City Board of Education. She in turn took it up with other educators, and the result was a luncheon meeting on March 8, 1962, in Sarnoff's private dining room, where seven New York public school officials discussed the idea and agreed unanimously that the city school system and RCA would formulate a pilot program to operate during the 1962-63 school year. Thus the David Sarnoff Industry-Science Teaching Program came into being.

Its aims are simple, but exciting and far-reaching. It will demonstrate how student interest in science studies and science careers can be increased through classroom presentations and after-school demonstration lectures by scientists and engineers from industry. The job of these industry representatives is to project the present and future horizons of science and technology in their own special fields.

At the end of the school year, results were then evaluated by the Office of Science Education and the Bureau of Educational Research of the school system, and further plans made.

There must be thousands of scientists, Sarnoff is certain, who would be glad to give a few hours of time a week to schools in their own communities, and he thinks the companies ought to be happy, in their own self-interest if for no other reason, to pay the cost.

In a young man's equipment for a successful life, using "success" in the Sarnoff sense, there must be more than knowledge, however; there must also be wisdom, and he makes a distinction between them. "I believe that knowledge is not necessarily a guarantee of wisdom," he says. "Some people who have very little knowledge have a great deal of wisdom, and some people who have a very great deal of knowledge have very little wisdom. It doesn't mean that knowledge is unimportant, or that wisdom would not be helped by knowledge. But wisdom is the combination of experience with life, the attitude of man towards man; it is human understanding; it is character; it is a combination of many things. To know how another person is going to react to a given situation is a product of wisdom, not of knowledge."

The General thinks we have lost in wisdom during the past 2,500 years while we have gone forward in knowledge; and the wisdom we have lost, he adds, lies in our failure to appreciate the fundamental values of life. "The things that we regard as most important today are not as wise as the things that were regarded most important in the past. Our present preoccupations more and more revolve upon our achievements, status, and what other people think of us. Learning, understanding and spiritual development are not as apparent today. The people of the past were more concerned with spiritual and ethical and moral concepts than they were with particular things."

Sarnoff is not one to grieve over the lost past, however. He admits that there are no modern equivalents of Plato, Aristotle, and Socrates around today; and when we talk of wisdom now, we always seem to find it in the mind of someone long dead. Nevertheless, wisdom will not be dead as long as young minds are trained and directed to absorb today's knowledge, with their eyes set toward the future and their heads in the stars. That is where the Sarnoff eyes and head have been all these years.

Chapter 9

A Look at the Future

To look at the future with David Sarnoff is not only to marvel at the technological wonders awaiting us, if the world solves its political and social problems, but to realize how a mind keyed to the future can never be satisfied with the frontiers of the present. It is a reminder, too, that the frontiers are always advancing.

As a young man growing up, Sarnoff confronted a world in 1906, when he got his first full-time job, whose citizens could not even imagine the world of the jet airplane and satellite communication that we know today. But in a half-dozen countries there were men like Sarnoff who looked beyond the limitations of the moment, who imagined and dreamed about what *could* be, and who constantly sought ways to make the future they visioned come true.

That is the reminder Sarnoff likes to make to young people today: the frontiers are always moving ahead and today man is only on the threshold of entirely new technologies. The wonders the world knows today are only the developmental forms of the wonders of tomorrow. Some of those wonders may be still only half-formed ideas in the mind of a boy somewhere today.

"The very fact that electronics and atomics are unfolding simultaneously is a portent of the amazing changes ahead," the General observes. "Never before have two such mighty forces been unleashed at the same time. Together they are certain to dwarf the industrial revolutions brought about by steam and electricity. There is no element of material progress we know today —in the biological and chemical fields, in atomics and electronics, in engineering and physics—that will not seem, from the vantage point of 1980, a fumbling prelude. . . .

"Not labor but leisure will be the great problem in the decades ahead. That prospect should be accepted as a God-given opportunity to add dimensions of enjoyment and grace to life. We have reason to foresee a fantastic rise in demand for, and appreciation of, the better, and perhaps the best, in art, music and letters.

"The job ahead is to assimilate scientific progress, to turn every potential for human benefit into a living reality."

Sarnoff distinguishes between discovery and invention. He thinks of himself as a discoverer, and, like

Columbus peering hopefully at the horizon, he sees a New World ahead. What will it be like? That is the General's favorite topic of conversation. In hundreds of interviews, speeches, and statements he has outlined the shape of the world of tomorrow, speaking with the authority of one who has been an accurate forecaster of things to come for more than 50 years. Bringing his vision of the future into focus, here is the world he envisions in the next two decades, give or take a few years.

Global television, already a reality, will be perfected and seen in full color, using the system of orbiting satellites which Telstar and Relay had presaged. When this system is in full and satisfactory operation, there will be no potentially fatal delays in communications like that which plagued President Kennedy in exchanging messages with Chairman Khrushchev at the time of the Cuban crisis. Instead, national leaders everywhere will be able to sit in their offices and speak to each other face to face through satellite television. Moreover, they will be able to understand each other instantly through automatic electronic translators.

There is television transmission today in 76 countries of the world, and more than 125,000,000 receivers in use. In 10 years, Sarnoff foresees, if the present growth continues, nearly every nation on earth will be telecasting, and there will be 200,000,000 receivers bringing what is telecast to an audience of 1,000,-000,000 people. All these people could be watching at the same time, and simultaneous translation techniques would make it understandable to every listener. Obviously, in a world in which nearly half the population is illiterate or semiliterate, nothing else will or could equal the impact of television on the human mind.

Sarnoff recognizes that this breathtaking aspect of the future is subject to political considerations. The receiving sets are non-ideological, like the satellite relay system, but whether there will be freedom to look and listen depends on mankind's ability to establish that freedom. Characteristically, the General has already proposed some radically new approaches.

One is the use of television for summit conferences among world leaders, employing the medium in the same way telephone conference calls are handled now. "We can visualize," Sarnoff says, "each national leader sitting in his television-equipped office—in London, Paris, Bonn, Moscow, Washington, or elsewhere. A television camera trained on each man will relay his image to all the others for viewing on a split screen or on multiple screens. In addition to conversing back and forth, each will be able to display charts or diagrams, or even films, relating to the questions on the prearranged agenda and he will see those which any of his conferees wish to project.

"When closed sessions are desired, the television transmissions could be scrambled and decoded by special equipment at each capital, using the same security techniques now widely employed in military and some commercial communications. When there was no need for secrecy, the conferences could be available for all to see and hear. With people everywhere riveted to the television screen, the leader of a Closed Nation might well think twice before blacking out his own country from an event of such magnitude—and one in which he himself participated."

But it will be important, Sarnoff believes, to establish a *continuing* global television project of compelling importance, and the answer to that may well be making a channel available for use by the United Nations when the satellite communications system is functioning. Then the only existing world forum where ideas are publicly exchanged and debated could be seen in all its strengths and shortcomings by the people everywhere who make it possible.

In the field of atomic science and electronics, the possibilities are almost limitless. Sarnoff himself has already transmitted radio messages through a device using a tiny atom-powered battery as its power source, but that is only a fractional beginning. Atomic waste products, already a problem in industry, could be used by homeowners as a power source. These products, sealed and buried in one small container under a house, could provide all the power needed by an average household for a period of 20 years. Similarly, atomic fuels extracted from relatively inexpensive materials are certain to be used everywhere in industry, and in all kinds of transportation—airplanes, trains, ships,

[167]

and automobiles. If this sounds visionary, Sarnoff merely points out that the direct conversion of atomic energy into electricity has already been demonstrated experimentally by RCA.

The prospects for nuclear fuels in transportation are particularly exciting. Both jet and rocket-type vehicles using these fuels will be capable of speeds as high as 5,000 miles per hour, and with greater safety and comfort than is known today. The cities of the world will be only a few hours apart—in some cases, commuting distance. The inexpensive personal airplane will come into its own and revolutionize travel, just as Henry Ford's flivver did at the beginning of this century. While aircraft will span the continents, automatically piloted, guided missiles will be transporting mail and freight all over the world.

Solar energy, in its way, will be as important as nuclear energy. The sun's rays will be harnessed and made to serve man, particularly in tropical and semi-tropical regions, where most of the developing nations lie. Solar power will be the answer for these nations, which now cannot afford to utilize fully the present fuels and sources of power.

Sarnoff has no fear of the effects of automation, which are already being felt by the American economy. Instead, he predicts automation will "reach a crescendo under the impact of cheap and abundant power. It will increase production, decrease costs, and make more goods and services available to more people.

The transition will create problems of adjustment, but ultimately automation will free millions of people from arduous and hazardous work. It will increase employment, reduce hours of labor, and increase leisure."

Automation processes will be applied, among other things, to the new products that advances in chemistry will provide, and some of these are certain to be spectacular—new plastics and ceramics, new lubricants, new substances still in the laboratory, and all available to meet any possible specification that man can imagine.

Illumination will be revolutionized by electroluminescence, or cold light, which is even now emerging from the laboratories. It provides light without heat, almost without shadow. Its glow will be easily controlled to provide any nuance of intensity or color desired. It can only be imagined how the appearance of factories, streets, stores, highways, and homes will be changed by cold light. On the highway, especially, it will be important because its glareless quality will help to eliminate the perils of night driving and flying. Cold light will also give us brighter and larger television pictures. Before long it will replace the television tube completely, so that the picture of the future will be seen on a thin, flat-surfaced screen hung on the wall like a picture.

New developments in irrigation and flood control, along with solar energy, the electronic acceleration of germination and growth and new chemical and biological discoveries, will greatly expand the food resources of mankind. The oceans will be farmed efficiently for nutritive products. By this means it may be possible to provide the food required by our exploding world population. If political and economic problems can somehow be solved, it will be possible to eliminate famine from the world.

Human health will be immensely benefited by an alliance of biology, chemistry, and physics, using the new tools of electronics and atomics. This powerful complex will bring about an avalanche of improvements in preventive medicine, and in the diagnosis and treatment of human ills. Biochemistry will provide new drugs to control disease and sustain health, particularly in old age; consequently man can expect to see his life span extended even farther, and in another quarter-century life expectancy may well approach 100 years.

The housewife will not only be healthy, but she will no longer be burdened with routine chores. These chores will be pre-scheduled every day, with all the tasks performed electronically. Temperature, humidity, and velocity of air in every part of the house will be kept automatically at the desired level, day and night. Bacteria and other contaminations will be removed from the air. Cooking and dishwashing will be done electronically, and waste will be disposed of the same way. "Fortunately," Sarnoff adds wryly, "we shall continue to do our own eating."

As he controls the climate of his home, man will also control the climate outside it. Major steps will be taken to make and control weather as desired. Ice-bound ports will be unfrozen, icebergs melted. Storms, even those of hurricane intensity, will either be diverted from a destructive course or dissipated, although it is possible that another 20 years will see only substantial progress, not realization, in the achievement of complete weather control.

Electronics and computers will be married in an alliance that is going to revolutionize professional life, particularly that of doctors. Already Sarnoff visualizes a television Medical School of the World, with doctors from every country watching surgical operations, hearing lectures, and witnessing demonstrations by leading specialists. These will be telecast via closed-circuit television in full color. "Worldwide medical television," he says, "would permit a heart specialist in London to examine a patient, display on the television screen his X-rays and cardiograms, and discuss a diagnosis with heart men in New York, Paris, Berlin, anywhere."

Computers, with their electronic memories, will provide through the worldwide storage of information an instantaneous review of anything a doctor wants to know about new developments in his specialty. Other computers will store the medical records of every patient, everywhere. A physician in Seattle need only dial a patient's code number to get his complete medical history, although he may have been treated previously in New York, or even London.

[171]

RCA

With scale model of RCA synchronous satellite

[172]

Electronic devices like the one that presently keeps several hundred cardiac cases alive by stimulating weak heart muscles to pump regularly can also be applied elsewhere in the body. "Some day," Sarnoff says, "devices like this may operate other human organs—the lungs, for example, or the kidneys. In fact, it is probable that the time will come when there will be complete electronic substitutes for worn-out human parts."

Computers will serve other professions as well as the doctors. The world's great law libraries, for example, will be codified and programmed into a computer, and the information retrieved in any language a lawyer seeking information might speak. In international law, a lawyer in New York could find out instantly what laws, regulations, and court decisions were pertinent to any case anywhere in the world. Research scientists would be similarly benefited.

The ultimate in communications on earth, Sarnoff believes, will come when men anywhere can speak with each other face to face. "A man equipped with a vest-pocket receiver-transmitter will connect with a nearby switchboard and be able to see and hear another man, similarly equipped, anywhere in the world. The channels available for this run into billions, and each individual will have his own private frequency, just as he now has a telephone number."

Speaking to the National Press Club in 1961, Sarnoff startled his listeners, who are not easily startled, by producing a pocket-size color television set, with combination AM-FM radio—a mock-up put together by RCA's Advanced Design Center. It was, as he pointed out, the forerunner of a universal communications instrument.

"The date of its availability," he told the newspapermen, "depends upon the time required to learn how to reduce further the size of certain components. I am bold enough to predict that it will be several times smaller than this, and it will consist of both a receiver and a transmitter, radio, television, AM, FM, black-and-white, and color.

"This prototype model is a symbol of our reach for the diminutive. I believe you will someday see transmitter-receiver units a half or third the size of this. Each receiver will have a decoding unit, responsive to only one of a million or more arrangements of pulses sent out from a transmitter, which means that you can be called while you have this in your pocket. . . . With complete privacy, a foreign editor in his office will one day be able to see and talk with a foreign correspondent in an airplane over Tokyo, in a boat on the Red Sea, or in a tractor at the moon camp."

That day appeared considerably advanced only two years later, with new developments in the use of the intensely powerful light generator known as the laser, which is light amplification by stimulated emission and radiation. The laser can produce a hot, needle-like beam that has already been used in human surgery, and that has opened a whole new world to the communications industry. Several types of lasers are under development; some are already on the market.

What the laser means to universal communication is an infinite broadening of frequencies, hitherto limited by the fact that sound and sight transmission has been accomplished only through electromagnetic waves, of which there are a limited number. "The use of laser," Sarnoff told an interviewer in 1963, "will make available an unlimited number of frequencies, enough for everyone in the world. Such a system will be in use in the decade ahead."

Thus the rapid pace of technology, moving so fast now that the General's forecast of "some day" in 1961 had to be shortened to "the decade ahead" in 1963, as the result of only three years of development.

Man's conquest of space is presently engaging much of Sarnoff's attention. He sees it as the next step in communications: "We will achieve the *earthbound* ultimate when we have direct man-to-man communications, both sight and sound, to any place on earth, regardless of distance. And we will achieve the *universal* ultimate when we have man—and possibly other species of life—exchanging communications over distances of millions of miles."

Sarnoff sees the history of communications as having progressed through successive phases. Phase One was the establishing of communication between a fixed point on land and ships at sea, and between ships themselves, or between two land areas across the oceans.

With mock-up of pocket TV set with FM and AM radio

[176]

Today this phase has been extended to all kinds of moving vehicles in touch with fixed stations and relay points on land.

Phase Two brought voice and music to listeners through radio broadcasting.

Phase Three brought what Sarnoff calls "a stretch-out of sight"—that is, black-and-white and then color television.

Phase Four is global television, and the problem there is no longer one of "how" but of "when."

Phase Five will be directed to communications with the moon and beyond. "Here," says Sarnoff, "we will be concerned initially with communications as a control and intelligence mechanism. This function will be crucial to the successful placing of men on the moon and, ultimately, on distant planets."

RCA has developed its own concept of a moon shot. It envisages the establishment of a well stocked camp on the moon before the first man gets there. The camp would have food, water, power, laboratory equipment, an exploration vehicle, appropriate emergency survival tools, and a reentry capsule for the manned trip back to earth.

The General describes this operation further: "A combination of a Saturn rocket and ground control devices should make it possible to put on the moon's surface a roving vehicle and to conduct a survey for the most appropriate area for a manned landing. This would be based on such factors as terrain, illumination, temperature, and other environmental characteristics. Then, through a series of subsequent Saturn shots, the camp could be established by sending up the necessary equipment and supplies, including a moon-crawling tractor for assembly purposes. This entire operation could be checked out by instrumentation controlled from the ground before we commit men to lunar flight.

"The success of this plan would prepare the way for exploration of the nearest planets. It would establish a pattern for the construction of other advance bases. In addition, validation of the techniques for storing fuel and refueling vehicles on the moon would lay an effective foundation for use of the moon itself as a launching platform for spacecraft."

Exploring the surface of the moon, Sarnoff believes, would establish whether it was practical to install an interplanetary radio relay station, controlled from the earth and intended to provide communications and navigational links for space vehicles. In spite of the unknown quantities involved—the nature of the moon's surface, radiation hazard from solar flares, the effect of the moon's environment on materials—Sarnoff believes that, in general, "the communications and control problems in this concept fall within our present capabilities."

Phase Five would be complete with sound-and-sight satellites in orbit around the earth, and electronic channels opened to the planets—a long way from the man-to-man communications of Phase One.

Phase Six would complete the circle: direct man-to-man, sight-and-sound communications over the ultimate in distances.

The speed with which these later phases will be accomplished depends in large part on the further progress of miniaturization, the shrinking of electronic gear. RCA has already made striking progress in that field. "Through formidable advances in micromodules," the General reports, "we are achieving new diminutives daily. We can now foresee a computer so compact that it will have a density equivalent to 100,-000,000 active elements per cubic foot—a density approaching the compactness of the human brain itself. And this computer, indeed, will perform many functions of the brain."

As exploration develops, space will become a vital factor in the national economy, perhaps the dominant one, Sarnoff believes. He points out that more than 5,000 companies and research organizations are already engaged in civilian and military space activities. They produce, among them, more than 3,200 different products related to space. All the major industries are involved in such production.

To doubters who believe the conquest of space is much farther away than these prophecies, the General recalls that only a little more than 60 years ago, when he came to this country, the telephone was a rarity, the Wright brothers' first successful experiment with the airplane was still three years in the future, and Marconi had not yet received his first historic wireless message across the Atlantic. Then he tells a story to illustrate the impact that science in recent developments has made upon time.

"I was traveling by train from New York to Washington, to a White House meeting with President Kennedy. It was the day Colonel John Glenn made the first orbit around the earth. I walked from the compartment to the dining car at the other end of the train, and in the few minutes this required, Colonel Glenn had flown a distance of some 2,500 miles—from the Hawaiian Islands to the Pacific Coast. In the length of time it took me to travel between my home and Washington, Colonel Glenn had flown 81,000 miles in space, at a speed of 17,500 miles an hour. And I was tuned in to virtually every minute of his flight, by home television, car radio, pocket radio on the train, and hotel television. Not even the most imaginative of science fiction writers could have depicted this reality 50 or even 30 years ago."

Sarnoff is well aware that the primary hindrance to the realization of the world he envisions is political rather than technological, and he has evolved a bold and comprehensive plan to organize and make effective the scientific resources of the free world in changing human life for the better, thus providing a climate of opinion on the globe virtually unassailable. In brief, totalitarian countries would have to "jine us" because they couldn't "lick us."

The General first offered this idea at the golden anniversary banquet of the Institute of Radio Engineers, in New York, in 1962. He proposed an organization to be called The Free World Community of Science, "an organization where competence is the only visa, and capabilities are fitted together for maximum results without regard to nationality." Initially it would embrace the nations of Western Europe, North and South America, Australia, and Japan, although any country permitting free scientific inquiry unhampered by political ideology would be welcome.

This Community of Science would include scientific leaders from the major areas of the physical and life disciplines from all the participating nations. Once established on a permanent basis, it would propose key areas of research, initiate specific research and development projects, and coordinate the resources essential to implement them. Wherever desirable, it would create specialized international research institutes. Functioning with a minimum of political direction, it would be supported financially by funds from the member nations.

In proposing the Community of Science, Sarnoff characteristically outlined the specific tasks he thought it could perform right away. He grouped these research areas into five broad categories, and in them provided still another look into the future.

1. Genetics and heredity. "We have begun the assault on the innermost mysteries of the life process—

decoding the nucleic structure of the living cell, its activities, differentiations, and transmitted characteristics. Knowledge of these basic life functions might make it possible ultimately to alter or modify cellular structures. This action could lead in turn to the elimination of bacterial or viral diseases, and conceivably to more useful strains of plant and animal life."

2. Communications and space. In this, his own area of primary interest, Sarnoff visioned again his system of interconnected high-level and low-level satellites, ground stations, and networks to provide every kind of communication to every place on earth, to space vehicles and the planets beyond. He cited, too, the promise of global weather control.

3. Conversion of saline to fresh water. "Two-thirds of the peoples of the earth live in areas that are water-starved. For millions of them, the presence of a few feet of water spells the difference between life, bare existence, or death. The nations which offer an efficient, low-cost process for large-scale purification of salt or brackish water will possess a weapon as potent as space ships in the battle for men's allegiance."

4. New sources of food. Here Sarnoff emphasizes the possibilities of a "harvest of the sea," which presently provides less than one per cent of the human diet. "The oceans offer an immediate challenge to our proposed Community of Science for improving food supplies by transforming fishing from a nomadic pursuit to an organized farming activity, including the scien-

tific processing of highly nutrient algae and plankton for food purposes."

5. New sources of energy. "Research in atomics, electronics, and other fields is now providing us with the means to convert solar energy, fossil fuel energy, and atomic fission energy directly into electric power. And through further research we shall ultimately learn how to make practical use of nuclear energy. When that day comes, we shall be able to tap the limitless energy sources in the oceans.

"Before too long, many isolated parts of the world will have sources of electricity that will not require large central power stations and extensive transmission systems. When we learn how to convert all forms of matter into energy for practical uses, we will have at our disposal the maximum force in nature. It will then be possible to cleave new coastlines, level mountain ranges, and transform the Sahara or our Southwestern deserts into irrigated gardens."

As an added fillip to his vast, imaginative plan, Sarnoff has suggested the establishment of an international data processing center to assemble, digest, translate, and make available the essential data in the technical papers published around the world, which in one year alone (1962) approached 60,000,000 pages.

In visioning the new world of research and technology that is only now dawning, the General has also from time to time thought of it in terms of its other problems—the common problems that all mankind

[183]

faces, in one way or another. These are his beliefs about the way these problems will be resolved in the next 20 years:

Communism will collapse in that time, he believes, because of "its economic fallacies, its political follies, and the pressures of a restive, discontented population." These pressures will be generated by the rise and spread of education, and the Soviet empire will come apart piecemeal as one satellite after another liberates itself. The Kremlin hierarchy itself will dissolve through internal struggles for power. A military dictatorship will replace it temporarily, to be followed by representative government.

Concurrently with this collapse, the Marxist approach to the solving of social problems will decline in the rapidly developing world of technology, and be replaced everywhere by the dynamics of a people's capitalism within a democratic framework.

Living standards without a parallel in the past will be attained all over the world as technical developments create an era of relative economic abundance. Leisure, not labor, will be the problem.

Economic progress and the new leisure will mean that man will enter a period of universal education. As general levels of knowledge rise, the new technology will place a premium on brains—that is, a need for ever more skilled scientists, engineers, designers, technicians, and others. But as this mounting demand enlarges educational facilities, the arts will be promoted as well as science, as man finds fresh channels for expression.

Every kind of entertainment will be available at home, both live *and* recorded, through television, radio, the phonograph, and electronic photography. Consequently there will be more opportunity than has ever been known for creative and interpretive talents. Programming will embrace everything created by the human mind.

In the field of government, public opinion will be a more decisive element in political life because people will have an unprecedented access to information. Electronic devices will quickly and accurately register the prevailing sentiment on any issue. Thus government and the governed will be brought ever more closely together, and popular government and democratic processes will thus be increasingly effective and efficient.

On the question that is foremost in everyone's mind, the possibility of nuclear war that would end all of mankind's hopes and aspirations, the General has this to say: "Universal communications and speedy transportation will shrink the world to a neighborhood. Technological developments in weapons of mass destruction will leave no doubt that the alternative is between survival or annihilation. All nations will find it imperative to develop and adopt practical means for disarmament based on effective inspection, control, and enforcement. War as an instrument of national policy will be outlawed."

[185]

The fantastic, almost overwhelming new world that the General envisages will be the inheritance of today's young people, who will also be the principal shapers of it. The General knows that it will not be easy for them. They will be growing up in years of extraordinary change that will mean serious dislocations of long established patterns of living. Already, in their brief lifetimes, they have seen a tremendous surge in science and technology that has already affected nearly every aspect of human existence.

There is, Sarnoff notes, a general apprehension among young people about how they will fit into the new age of technology. It is more acute, perhaps, among those whose bent is not toward science. Some of the more perceptive high school and college students miss and even envy the seeming certainties of the past, although they may not have personally experienced but only read about them. This feeling has led to a conservative trend among them not typical of youth.

Oddly enough, with so much to be done in the world, many young people today appear to wonder what more is left to accomplish. "I have talked with a great many young people," Sarnoff says, "and some of them have frankly sought advice on their careers and opportunities. On occasion they expressed the fear, like Alexander the Great, that there may be no more worlds to conquer."

It is true that the last of our geographical frontiers disappeared with the present exploration of the Antarctic. The electron and the atom are in the process of being harnessed. Individual skill seems to have lost some of its old importance. The conquest of space moves forward so rapidly that the basic tasks—some young men and women fear—may soon be fulfilled.

Sarnoff's answer to such doubts is unequivocal: "We are only on the threshold of knowledge about the universe that will open up new opportunities for youth and for the advancement of all mankind." It is not only the number and variety of discoveries and inventions in our era that guarantee this promise, the General points out, but the speed of new developments. Scientific progress has accelerated at a dizzying speed, as the events of his own lifetime prove. The technical changes in that period were greater than those made in the 20 centuries that went before. At the present rate, the next decade may well see more change than the five decades preceding it. New words and formulas have to be improvised to keep pace; man's vocabulary of measurement is constantly outmoded. He has had to devise the word *megaton,* for example, to indicate the rough equivalent of 1,000,000 tons of TNT. Similarly the speeds of sound and light were once used only to measure natural phenomena; now they are commonplace measurements of man-made phenomena.

What the young people are feeling today, Sarnoff thinks, is simply another reflection of the feeling adults have—that man has extended his mastery over the material world but is losing mastery over himself. As Albert Schweitzer put it: "Man has learned to control the forces of nature before he has learned to control himself."

Believing that unless we close this gap man will find himself the slave and not the master of the powers he has summoned, Sarnoff asserts: "It is in this reality, in this threat, that one must look for answers to the question raised by young people. An immense amount of vital and rewarding work remains for them to accomplish in order to bring humanity into harmonious relation with its shifting material environment.

"We have built up a staggering storehouse of knowledge about the world around us, but man himself is still shrouded in a smog of misconception and ignorance. We have learned to identify with uncanny accuracy the chemical composition of stardust millions of miles away, but still know relatively little about the composition of cancer cells in our own bodies.

"More important, though man has understood the complexities of the atom, he has largely failed to understand his fellow man. He has learned to see and hear electronically to the outer reaches of space, yet his mind has been unable to cross the narrow boundaries of prejudice.

"More than ever before, therefore, we must give thought to the wisdom of the ancient Greek injunction: 'Man, know thyself!' More than ever before, we must act on the truth that the proper study of man is man himself."

The time has come, the General believes, for a penetrating study of man in all his dimensions, both physical and metaphysical. There must be a concentrated study of body, mind, and soul. As he puts it, "Our preoccupation with *outer* space must be balanced with a purposeful exploration of *inner* space."

That, he conceives, is the paramount task awaiting youth today: "To learn as much about the *Adam* as the older generation has learned about the *Atom*. There are worlds to be opened up and charted *within* ourselves, as exciting as any that we have tackled *outside* ourselves."

What are some of these inner worlds? The mysteries of our bodies constitute one of them. In spite of everything medicine has done to conquer or control so many once fatal diseases, and to improve our health generally, every doctor knows the truth of the remark made recently by Dr. James Watt, head of the National Heart Institute, when he said: "We have blazed a long trail but an uncharted wilderness lies ahead." For example, we know little of the great arterial system that gives us life, and the brain in which it is rooted. We know even less of what causes the sick minds that fill half the hospital beds in this country. More Americans go into hospitals with mental illness than with all the other diseases put together.

Electronics will be the useful tool of the young men and women who go into medicine, as it already is in so many ways. But Sarnoff would not be Sarnoff if he did not suggest a device still in the future which will be of use to everyone. He says: "Our automobiles and airplanes have dashboards of gauges and meters that give the driver or pilot all the pertinent information about the operating parts and behavior. There is no technical reason why we cannot develop an equivalent 'dashboard' for the human body. It will be a home device, like scales, that will register not only weight but heartbeats, blood pressure, pulse rate, temperature and other basic data. Moreover, it will carry an alarm system advising the user when to consult a physician. The same device will record the daily results on magnetic tape to help the doctor in his diagnosis."

But there is a need to explore the inner man in more than a physical sense. Man must be comprehended as a social, intellectual, and spiritual entity, a job more important and formidable than learning about his physical makeup. Only through such comprehension can we cultivate to its fullest extent the human potential on which our civilization rests.

That prospect excites Sarnoff as much as the idea of radio and television excited him long ago. "This difficult assignment," he said recently, "is replete with the kind of adventures of discovery to stir the imagination of our ablest young people. Human motives, instincts, impulses and behavior patterns have, for the most part, eluded the analysts and statisticians. Vision is clouded by racial and religious animosities unrelated to reason. Too often a sense of purpose is lost in a hurricane of irrational passions. The possibilities for devoted labor in this area are almost limitless."

Such problems require as much courage, imagination, and zeal as any of the geographical or technological frontiers crossed in the past. Once he becomes aware of this challenge, Sarnoff believes, no young student will have any reason to deplore a lack of worlds to conquer. More than that, the General charges youth with direct and personal responsibility for preserving the core values of civilization, and the principles that give meaning to life.

What of Sarnoff now in his 70's, a man who has done so much, seen so much, knows so much? What more—echoing the anxious question of his young friends—is there left for him to accomplish? His answer is characteristically tough and wise, and good enough to guide a young man from his youth to old age: "First you're an apprentice. Then you're an actor on the stage. Then you sit in the audience and applaud. I want to help those around me who have ideas. I've reached the 'audience' stage, but I'm not content merely to applaud."

If there is a single lesson to be learned from David Sarnoff's valuable life, this may well be it: Never be content merely to applaud. That is only for the present. The pursuit is always toward the horizon, toward the challenge and the promise of the future. "Learn from the past," David Sarnoff advises, "do your best in the present, and dream and plan for a better future."

AT THE WILL
OF THE BODY

Arthur W. Frank

AT THE WILL
OF THE BODY

Reflections on Illness

HOUGHTON MIFFLIN COMPANY

Boston 1991

For information about permission to reproduce selections from
this book, write to Permissions, Houghton Mifflin Company,
2 Park Street, Boston, Massachusetts 02108.

Library of Congress Cataloging-in-Publication Data

Frank, Arthur W.
At the will of the body : reflections on illness /
Arthur W. Frank.
p.   cm.
ISBN 0-395-56188-4
1. Frank, Arthur W. — Health.   2.   Cancer — Patients —
United States — Biography.   3.   Heart — Infarction —
Patients — United States — Biography.   4.   Sick —
Psychology.   I.   Title.
RC265.6.F73A3   1991
616'.001'9 — dc20   90-4459
[B]   CIP

Printed in the United States of America

AGM 10 9 8 7 6 5 4 3 2 1

The quotation from *The Illness Narratives*, by Arthur Kleinman,
M.D., copyright © 1988 by Basic Books, Inc., is reprinted by
permission of Basic Books, Inc., Publishers, New York. The quotation from *Diary of a Zen Nun*, by Nan Shin, © 1986, is reprinted by permission of E. P. Dutton, Inc. The quotation from
"Author's Notes to *The Marriage of Bette and Boo*," by Christopher Durang, published by Dramatists Play Service, is reprinted
by permission of the author. The lyrics from "The Boy in the
Bubble" and "Crazy Love," copyright © 1986 Paul Simon, are
reprinted by permission of Paul Simon Music. The lines from
"Gravy," by Raymond Carver, are from the book *A New Path to
the Waterfall*, copyright © 1989 by the estate of Raymond Carver,
and are used by permission of Atlantic Monthly Press. The lines
from *Tao Te Ching*, by Lao Tzu, translated by Stephen Mitchell,
copyright © 1988 by Stephen Mitchell, are reprinted by permission of HarperCollins Publishers.

To Cathie,

who joins me in remembering

LAURA IRENE FOOTE

1928–1988

and

BARBARA ANN WANNER

1942–1988

ACKNOWLEDGMENTS

Many people influenced this book. I thank them for what they have been to me, but I limit myself to naming those who directly affected the manuscript. My agent, Doe Coover, anticipated what the project was about and helped me hold onto my sense of purpose. The editorial care of Henry Ferris, of Houghton Mifflin, is apparent in every paragraph, if not every line. Peg Anderson, my manuscript editor, clarified my thoughts and intentions throughout. My thanks also to Larry Platt for his assistance with the book's production.

What I know of illness I have learned together with my wife, Catherine Foote. This is our book, no less than they were our illnesses.

CONTENTS

It is possible to talk with patients, even those who are most distressed, about the actual experience of illness. . . . Witnessing and helping to order that experience can be of therapeutic value.

Arthur Kleinman, The Illness Narratives

And someone else wrote me, "What I want is to know your own experience of illness."
Why the interest?
People on their ailments are not always interesting, far from it. But we all hope for a — must I say the word — recipe, we all believe, however much we know we shouldn't, that maybe somebody's got that recipe and can show us how not to be sick, suffer and die.

Nan Shin, Diary of a Zen Nun: Every Day Living

Unless you go through all the genuine angers you feel, both justified and unjustified, the feelings of love that you do have will not have any legitimate base and will be at least partially false. Plus, eventually you will go crazy.

Christopher Durang, "Author's Notes to
The Marriage of Bette and Boo"

Illness as a
Dangerous Opportunity

I HAVE EXPERIENCED life-threatening illness twice. I had a
heart attack when I was thirty-nine and cancer at age forty.
Now that these illnesses are in remission, why go back and
write about them? Because illness is an opportunity, though a
dangerous one. To seize this opportunity I need to remain
with illness a little longer and share what I have learned
through it.

Critical illness offers the experience of being taken to the
threshold of life, from which you can see where your life could
end. From that vantage point you are both forced and allowed
to think in new ways about the value of your life. Alive but
detached from everyday living, you can finally stop to consider why you live as you have and what future you would
like, if any future is possible. Illness takes away parts of your
life, but in doing so it gives you the opportunity to choose the
life you will lead, as opposed to living out the one you have
simply accumulated over the years.

The most obvious danger of disease is that you will continue
over the threshold and die. This danger is paramount, and at

some time it will be unavoidable. The danger you can avoid is that of becoming attached to illness, using it to withdraw from encountering yourself and others. Illness is something to recover from if you can, but recovery is worth only as much as what you learn about the life you are regaining.

Recovery has different meanings. After my heart attack it meant putting the whole experience behind me. I wanted to return to a place in the healthy mainstream as if nothing had happened. Cancer does not allow that version of recovery. I am reminded, every time I see a doctor or fill out an insurance form, that there is no "cure" for cancer, only remission. But more important than the physiology of the disease is the impact of the experience. After cancer I had no desire to go back to where I was before. The opportunity for change had been purchased at too great a cost to let it slip away. I had seen too much suffering from a perspective that is often invisible to the young and the healthy. I could not take up the same game in the old terms. I wanted less to recover what I had been than to discover what else I might be. Writing is part of this discovery.

A problem with the view of recovery as the ideal ending of illness is that some people do not recover. Soon after my treatment for cancer ended, my wife, Cathie, and I returned to the cancer center to be with her mother, whose illness ended in her death at fifty-nine. If recovery is taken to be the ideal, how is it possible to find value in the experience of an illness that either lingers on as chronic or ends in death? The answer seems to be in focusing less on recovery and more on renewal. Even continuing illness and dying contain opportunities for renewal.

To seize the opportunities offered by illness, we must live illness actively: we must think about it and talk about it, and some, like me, must write about it. Through thinking, talking, and writing we can begin, as individuals and as a society, to accept illness fully. Only then can we learn that it is nothing special. Being ill is just another way of living, but by the time we have lived through illness we are living differently. Because illness can lead us to live differently, accepting it is neither easy nor self-evident. I write about illness to work out some terms in which it can be accepted. I want to enter into the experience of illness and witness its possibilities, but not so far as to become attached to being ill. Seizing the opportunity means experiencing it fully, then letting go and moving on.

This book began during my illnesses in conversations and in letters. Of all the care Cathie gave me, the most important was her willingness and ability to talk about what was happening to me and to her. Through our talk illness did not happen just to me, it happened to us. My sense of being part of a larger "us" developed in letters I exchanged with friends and relatives, some of whom had been critically ill themselves. The circle expanded to books by others about their illnesses. Ultimately, as in all experience, no clear line marks off what is "mine" from what I have lived through others.

One letter in particular gave me the start I needed to write this book. A cousin asked me to write to a friend of hers, a man who had lung cancer. Writing to someone you do not know about something as personal as cancer is not easy. But I knew how much it had meant to me, when I was ill, to receive letters from persons willing to become involved in my experience and offering their own experiences to me. When I finally wrote the letter to my cousin's friend, I realized it only hinted at topics needing much more discussion.

I want what I have written to be touched as one touches letters, folding and refolding them, responding to them. I hope ill persons will talk back to what I have written. Talking back is how we find our own experiences in a story someone else has written. The story I tell is my own, but readers can add their lives to mine and change what I have written to fit their own situations. These changes can become a conversation between us.

Too many ill persons are deprived of conversation. Too many believe they cannot talk about their illness. By talk about illness, I do not mean explanations of their diagnoses and treatment. What most ill persons say about their illness comes from their physicians and other medical staff, not from themselves. The ill person as patient is simply repeating what has been said elsewhere — boring second-hand medical talk. When ill persons try to talk in medicalese, they deny themselves the drama of their personal experience.

Ill persons have a great deal to say for themselves, but rarely do I hear them talk about their hopes and fears, about what it is like to be in pain, about what sense they make of suffering and the prospect of death. Because such talk embarrasses us, we do not have practice with it. Lacking practice, we find such talk difficult. People then believe that illness is not something to talk about. They miss the opportunity of learning to experience it with another. Renewal is easiest if it is a shared process.

What I have to tell relates no cures I have discovered or medical miracles. I got sick, went through the prescribed treatments, engaged in my share of obnoxious behavior, managed to cope, and lived to tell the tale. This tale will not tell anyone how to cope, but it does bear witness to what goes into coping. That witness, I believe, is enough.

I am not an inspiring case, only a writer. By profession I am a university professor, a sociologist with additional training and experience in philosophy, communications, and psychotherapy. These resources helped me put my experiences into words. But I do not write as any kind of expert; I present myself only as a fellow sufferer, trying to make sense of my own illness. If I sometimes seem to offer advice, it is only that I am being carried away in my attempt to share experience. I cannot tell people how to be sick any more than I can say how to get well. I can only witness some of the realities of illness.

This book offers starting points for talking and thinking about illness. My own experiences are in no sense a recipe for what others can expect or should experience. I know of no exemplary way to be ill. We all have to find our own way, but we do not necessarily have to be alone. I can write about where I encountered problems and where I found moments of value. Ill persons can hold out these examples of illness experience to family, friends, and medical staff as proof of all there is to talk about. Talk is not the only way to elevate illness beyond pain and loss, but for most people it may be the most reliable way. For those who read this book alone, I hope it will be a good partner in silent conversation. I hope that for most it will be the beginning of conversation with others.

I write first to those who are now ill, but not just to them. Since we all will become ill someday, other readers may find this book useful as a way of considering what that will mean.

I write also to those who care for the ill. Caregivers are the other halves of the conversations I encourage the ill to engage in. They are also the other halves of illness experiences. The care they give begins by doing things for ill persons, but it turns into sharing the life they lead. I hope I suggest something of what there is to be shared.

Since my own experience comprises heart attack and cancer, I write about these illnesses. Cancer gets more attention, not only because my experiences were more extensive, but because social attitudes toward cancer are more complex. Despite this focus, I hope readers experiencing or concerned with other illnesses will not feel excluded. Different diseases set in place different possibilities, but there remains a common core of what critical illness does to a life.

Critical illness leaves no aspect of life untouched. The hospitals and other special places we have constructed for critically ill persons have created the illusion that by sealing off the ill person from those who are healthy, we can also seal off the illness in that ill person's life. This illusion is dangerous. Your relationships, your work, your sense of who you are and who you might become, your sense of what life is and ought to be — these all change, and the change is terrifying. Twice, as I realized how ill I was, I saw these changes coming and was overwhelmed by them.

So I write to the younger self I was before illness overwhelmed me. I write to a self not so many years younger but a gulf of experience away. In a short story by Jorge Luis Borges, the writer, now old, is sitting by a river. Along comes his younger self, out for a walk. They recognize each other and talk. The younger man is particularly shocked that the other is almost blind. The older man comforts him, telling him the condition is nothing to be feared. If my younger self met me now and heard what was to be his medical history, he would be even more shocked than Borges's younger self. In what follows I want to tell my self-before-illness that his fears are legitimate, but he would be a fool to spend his life being fearful. He will suffer and have losses, but suffering and loss are not incompatible with life.

For all you lose, you have an opportunity to gain: closer relationships, more poignant appreciations, clarified values. You are entitled to mourn what you can no longer be, but do not let this mourning obscure your sense of what you can become. You are embarking on a dangerous opportunity. Do not curse your fate; count your possibilities.

Becoming Ill

ONE DAY my body broke down, forcing me to ask, in fear and frustration, what's happening to me? Becoming ill is asking that question. The problem is that as soon as the body forces the question upon the mind, the medical profession answers by naming a disease. This answer is useful enough for practicing medicine, but medicine has its limits.

Medicine has done well with my body, and I am grateful. But doing *with* the body is only part of what needs to be done *for* the person. What happens when my body breaks down happens not just to that body but also to my life, which is lived in that body. When the body breaks down, so does the life. Even when medicine can fix the body, that doesn't always put the life back together again. Medicine can diagnose and treat the breakdown, but sometimes so much fear and frustration have been aroused in the ill person that fixing the breakdown does not quiet them. At those times the experience of illness goes beyond the limits of medicine.

The day I had a heart attack I could not imagine that my body was breaking down. I was thirty-nine years old and thinking about competing in a race the next day. It would be the first race of my tenth year of competitive recreational running. For much of the winter I had had a virus, but it was March, spring was beginning, and last week's cold seemed to be over. I went for a jog along the river behind our house. I was running easily, but my pulse seemed too fast. Passing a parking lot, I saw another runner getting out of his car and took the excuse to stop and talk. I leaned on the hood of his car, started to say something about my heart beating fast, and then woke up on the ground.

I had undergone what cardiologists would later call ventricular tachycardia. Simply put, my heart had sped up, beating erratically and uncontrollably fast, then had stopped for a moment. A year later my cardiologist would tell me I was lucky that my heart had started again and that it had not stopped long enough to cause permanent damage. But at the time I did not know what had happened. I had a scraped shin, and I felt shaky.

I got a ride home, took a shower, and that night I even went to a party. I was worried because I had never passed out before, but how serious could it be? I was an athlete, even if a middle-aged one. My mind wanted to forget it. My body said no. Something was wrong; something had changed, seriously. When I saw my family physician, he went along with my mind's version, dismissing what had happened but ordering a cardiogram just to be sure. A week later he called to tell me it showed I had had a heart attack. He seemed uncertain of the medical details, but I hardly heard him; I was lost in a sense of sudden and profound change. In the moments of that call I became a different person.

During that week I had been asking, what's happening to me? My physician provided the medical answer, but it has taken me years to understand why it was not *my* answer. My physician was a model of politeness. We spoke over the phone as professionals: he called me Dr. Frank, I called him Dr. ————. We talked about my heart as if we were consulting about some computer that was producing errors in the output. "It" had a problem. Our talk was classier than most of the conversations I have with the mechanic who fixes my car, but only because my doctor and I were being vague. He was not as specific as my mechanic usually is. I knew more about hearts than I knew about cars, but this engine was inside me, so I was even more reluctant to hear about the scope of the damage.

What was wrong with that conversation, for me as an ill person, was precisely what made my physician's performance so professional. To be professional is to be cool and management oriented. Professional talk goes this way: A problem seems to have come up, more serious than we thought, but we can still manage it. Here's our plan; any questions? Hearing this talk, I knew full well that I was being offered a deal. If my response was equally cool and professional, I would have at least a junior place on the management team. I knew that as a patient's choices go, it wasn't a bad deal, so I took it. I was even vaguely complimented.

I did not yet know the cost of taking that deal. Experiences are to be lived, not managed. The body is not to be managed, even by myself. My body is the means and medium of my life; I live not only in my body but also through it. No one should be asked to detach his mind from his body and then talk about this body as a thing, out there. No one should have to stay cool and professional while being told his or her body is breaking down, though medical patients always have to do just that. The demand being made of me was to treat the breakdown as if fear and frustration were not part of it, to act as if my life, the whole life, had not changed.

To others who have had or will have such a conversation, I must add that *I did not know what I wanted to say* or what I wanted the physician to say. I did not want to cry or scream or give a speech on the shortness of life. I'm not sure that what I wanted to say could be put into words. But I needed some recognition of what was happening to me. That day I became someone who had come very close to dying, and I might very soon come that close again. To become such a person is to change. After I heard that I had had a heart attack, how I lived in my body changed, and my doctor should have found a way to let me know he recognized that.

Being told I had had a heart attack required celebration. To celebrate is not necessarily to rejoice over an event but to mark its significance. A funeral celebrates a life. Tears and silence can celebrate an occasion just as kisses and handshakes do. But instead of my physician and I finding some terms to celebrate what was happening to me, we avoided recognizing the experience. We allowed ourselves to talk only about the mechanics of disease. I would have to learn to celebrate illness on my own.

The point is not that my physician was incompetent. On the contrary, he did exactly what professionals are trained to do. And I acted exactly as patients are trained to act. What is important for ill persons to understand is that there are limits to professional competence. Physicians too often do not express to the patient that they recognize her experiences of fear, frustration, and personal change. Their talk is about diseases, about the parts that have broken down, not about the whole, which is living that breakdown. But physicians' self-imposed limitations dictate the reciprocal roles patients are expected to play in responding to physicians. I was naive about physicians and illness and accepted these limitations. It thus took me much longer to recognize the power of illness to change my life and the way I think about myself.

The beginning of understanding was to recognize the difference between disease and illness. Medical talk uses disease terms that reduce the body to physiology, the organization of which can be measured. Disease terms include measures of body temperature, the presence or absence of infections, the circulation and composition of blood and other fluids, the texture of skin, and on and on. In disease talk these terms are used to indicate a breakdown, either present or imminent. Because the disease terms refer to measurements, they are "objective." Thus in disease talk *my* body, my ongoing experience of being alive, becomes *the* body, an object to be measured and thus objectified. "Objective" talk about disease is always medical talk. Patients quickly learn to express themselves in these terms, but in using medical expressions ill persons lose themselves: the body I experience cannot be reduced to the body someone else measures.

When a person becomes a patient and learns to talk disease talk, her body is spoken of as a place that is elsewhere, a "site" where the disease is happening. In speaking this way the patient identifies with the physician, for whom the patient's body *is* elsewhere. Since the ill person can see that it is far safer and more comfortable to be the physician, this confusion of identity is understandable, but it remains mistaken. The cost of this confusion to the ill person is forgetting that she exists as part of "it."

Illness is the experience of living through the disease. If disease talk measures the body, illness talk tells of the fear and frustration of being inside a body that is breaking down. Illness begins where medicine leaves off, where I recognize that what is happening to my body is not some set of measures. What happens to my body happens to my life. My life consists of temperature and circulation, but also of hopes and disappointments, joys and sorrows, none of which can be measured. In illness talk there is no such thing as *the* body, only *my* body as I experience it. Disease talk charts the progression of certain measures. Illness talk is a story about moving from a perfectly comfortable body to one that forces me to ask: What's happening to *me*? Not *it*, but *me*.

Medical treatment, whether in an office or hospital or on the phone, is designed to make everyone believe that only the disease — what is measurable and mechanical — can be discussed. Talking to doctors always makes me conscious of what I am *not* supposed to say. Thus I am particularly silent when I have been given bad news. I know I am supposed to ask only about the disease, but what I feel is the illness. The questions I want to ask about my life are not allowed, not speakable, not even thinkable. The gap between what I feel and what I feel allowed to say widens and deepens and swallows my voice.

Physicians are generally polite about answering questions,

but to ask a question one must already imagine the terms of an answer. My questions end up being phrased in disease terms, but what I really want to know is how to live with illness. The help I want is not a matter of answering questions but of witnessing attempts to live in certain ways. I do not want my questions answered; I want my experiences shared. But the stress and multiple demands on physicians and nurses too often push such sharing outside the boundaries of "professional" activity.

The more extreme the situation, the more time and help I need to say anything. When I face someone who does not seem willing or able to help me work toward what I might eventually say, I become mute. A person who finds no one willing to take the time and offer the help necessary to bring forth speech will protect himself by saying nothing. But the time when I cannot immediately put something into words is usually the time when I most need to express myself. Having no questions hardly means having nothing to say. You cannot be told that you have had a heart attack without having a great deal to express and needing to express it. The problem is finding someone who will help you work out the terms of that expression.

After five years of dealing with medical professionals in the context of critical illness, as opposed to the routine problems I had had before, I have accepted their limits, even if I have never become comfortable with them. Perhaps medicine should reform itself and learn to share illness talk with patients instead of imposing disease talk on them. Or perhaps physicians and nurses should simply do what they already do well — treat the breakdowns—and not claim to do more. This book will not resolve that question. What I offer ill persons is more immediate. Recognize that more is happening to you than you can discuss with most physicians in most medical settings. To talk about illness you must go elsewhere.

I have needed talk to express the changes that illness has brought to my life; through talk I continue to work out new ways of living with those changes. Critically ill persons need talk that recognizes all that they are experiencing. They need to talk not only for themselves, but also for those who are not yet ill. Illness can teach us all how to live a saner, healthier life. Illness is a threat to life, but it also witnesses what is worth living. However much suffering there is and however much we want to avoid being ill, we may need illness. Expressing that need, finding the terms in which to celebrate illness, is the task that lies head.

Illness as Incident

HEART PROBLEMS teach you how quickly life can go out of a body. My fear was that I would go to sleep and not wake up again. Having a heart attack is falling over the edge of a chasm and then being pulled back. Why I was pulled back made no more sense than why I fell in the first place. Afterward I felt always at risk of one false step, or heartbeat, plunging me over the side again. I will never lose that immanence of nothingness, the certainty of mortality. A heart attack is a moment of death. Once the body has known death, it never lives the same again.

People who think of themselves as healthy walk that edge too, but they see only the solid ground away from the chasm. Knowing that you walk on the edge is not just an experience of fear; it is also a clarification. I have hiked trails high in the Rocky Mountains, climbing through thick fog. At a certain altitude the fog clears, and suddenly I can see all that lies below me. It may be a long drop to the bottom, but the view is spectacular, and it is only at the moment of clearing that I know where I am.

I was not able to do much hiking in the period after my heart attack. Medicine's suspicion was that a viral infection had worked its way into my heart muscle. As a physician said to me, sometimes it's just a virus, sometimes you get myocarditis (an infection of the heart muscle), sometimes encephalitis (inflammation of the brain). When I heard this, my image of the path along the chasm's edge narrowed still further. I underwent a series of stress tests that monitored my heart while I ran on a treadmill. It was a relief to be running again, even in a hospital lab. The problem was that certain irregularities continued to show up in my heartbeat. My pulse rose much faster than it should have. My cardiologist could not rule out arterial blockage as the cause of my heart attack.

By September, six months after I had passed out, I felt better, but my stress tests were looking worse, and a decision was made to move on to the next diagnostic measure, an angiogram. This is a high-tech procedure in which a small incision is made near the groin and a catheter is passed through the vein into the heart. A dye is then injected into the heart through the catheter. The dispersion of the dye through the arteries is videotaped from X-ray monitors, and the cardiologist can locate any blockage. In addition, the rhythm of the heartbeat in the various chambers can be observed more closely than ultrasound procedures allow. The angiogram is done under local anesthetic, since the patient has to move around on command in order to get the proper X-ray angles.

The idea of having a catheter passed through a vein into my heart was mildly terrifying, though this part of the angiogram involved no sensation whatsoever. I had not looked forward to the procedure, but it was exciting. The injection of the dye produced a flush throughout my body that was almost pleasant enough to make up for the pinch of the initial incision. But the real excitement was on the television screen, where I watched my own heart beat and saw the dye spread out through the arteries.

At the time, however, I was less interested in seeing my heart than in knowing what the dispersion of the dye would show. Fortunately it showed a strong, regular heartbeat and no arterial blockage. For six months I had felt under a sentence of indeterminate doom. Hearing the cardiologist's immediate judgment of "good arteries" lifted that sentence. He went on to tell me that I could resume my normal athletic activities. I asked whether he would do any more stress tests, and he wisely replied no, he had a pretty good idea what they would show. Apparently running in hospital labs does not suit me; my heart wanted to get back outdoors. Outdoors I went, hardly looking back.

It would not be fair to myself to say I learned nothing from what happened. The next morning I had the thrill of remembering — as I remember it today — what my own heart looked like, beating on those television monitors. After months of staring at the abstract cardiograms of my heartbeat, here at last was a chance to see the real thing in action. Ours is the first age in history when people can look inside themselves and see their vital organs working. Even if that vision of inner space is mediated by a television screen, it is an adventure to behold. I had the sense to appreciate that.

Mostly, however, I wanted to escape from the world of illness and forget my view of the chasm. When I went for a final checkup several months later, my cardiologist told me I had been lucky that day in March; it could have ended differently. He also told me that if the virus recurred I would have a slightly increased immunity to it. Moreover, we now knew my arteries were in fine shape and, given my age, they would probably stay that way. I was more than willing to define what had happened as what medicine calls an "incident." It was a flat tire on the road of life, an annoying but minor breakdown. Some time had been lost, I had gotten a little dirty while repairs were made, but the tire was patched and I could continue the journey as if nothing had happened. It was only an incident, an interlude of no real consequence.

Some time later I read a wonderful passage by Robert Louis Stevenson in which he described his youthful travel in southern France: "And I blessed God that I was free to wander, free to hope, and free to love." After my cardiologist told me to resume my life without restriction or fear, there were no boundaries on what I felt free to do. Being pronounced cured did not restore me to my previous physical condition; I could still run only a hundred yards without losing my breath. But I was free to try whatever I wanted. I was even free not to look back on what had happened.

Illness is a restriction. At best it requires spending time in treatment and enduring limitations on one's activity. At worst it deforms and impairs the body and cages the mind. Whenever I walk out of a hospital or a doctor's office, some part of me repeats the Stevenson quotation, and I too bless God for my freedom. But if freedom requires good health, it is precarious indeed. My heart attack should have taught me how little control we have over the condition of our bodies. My "incident" was, so far as anyone knows, the luck of the viral dice, and my recovery was no less a matter of chance, a contingency.

Thinking of my heart attack as an incident left me free to wander, but that freedom was based on an illusion that my health was unassailable. I had had my one breakdown, and now I was entitled to smooth traveling for the rest of the trip. All I thought of those who were not set free from illness, whose luck was not so good, was "Poor devils." By denying what I ought to have learned about my own vulnerability, I left myself more vulnerable still.

We are vulnerable creatures; that is what we share as humans. Being free to wander, hope, and love does not mean denying our vulnerability; rather it means embracing it. Only when we act in full knowledge of our vulnerability do we learn to discriminate. This does not mean simply choosing to wander here rather than there, hoping for this and not that, loving one rather than another. It means finding at the core of each activity an affirmation of living that goes beyond the particular choices of where, what, and whom.

When we wander, hope, and love as an affirmation of life rather than as a pursuit of this or that choice, we no longer depend on good health. When I left that cardiologist's office I had not had enough bad health to know how or why this is so. Within the year I would learn that the ill or impaired may, in the sense of fulfilling life, be far more free than healthy people. The healthy require health as an affirmation that their will is still effective, and they must continually prove this effectiveness. The ill accept their vulnerability as an affirmation that the world is perfect without any exercise of their will, and this acceptance is their freedom. But to understand this I had to learn a different version of recovery, not from an incident but from an illness.

Defining my heart attack as an incident left me dependent on good health, which I once again assumed as my right. I still did not know how to enjoy health without making it a condition of my life. We are free only when we no longer require health, however much we may prefer it.

Becoming Ill Again

FIFTEEN MONTHS after my heart attack I was once again feeling healthy. In July I competed in a swim-bike-run triathlon, finished within a minute of my time two years earlier, and decided I was back where I had been. That was what I wanted from recovery — to get back to where I was before. But even in those terms, all was not well. When drying myself off after showering, I began to notice a persistent soreness in one testicle. Since childhood I have tended to have "swollen glands" as a response to viral infection, and at first I thought little of the soreness. As the discomfort increased I began to do what all men should do regularly: examine my testicles. I could feel a sharp ridge that had formed around the lower third of the left one. It felt as if the normal oval shape was turning into a figure eight, reminding me of the picture in my high school biology text of a cell about to divide. This was not what the testicle looked like but how it felt.

I suspected cancer because my "professional" training had given me the little bit of knowledge that, as the cliché correctly says, is a dangerous thing. When I was a graduate student in the early 1970s, I attended a seminar with a visiting sociologist whose specialty was epidemiology, the study of the distribution of diseases in geographical and social space. Social epidemiologists are particularly interested in how diseases vary by age, sex, race, and "social class" factors such as income, education, and type of employment. In the course of the seminar our visitor mentioned one of the most baffling diseases he had studied, cancer of the testes.

I had never heard of testicular cancer. While it came as no surprise that you could have cancer there, it was not what any man wants to hear. Most upsetting was the profile of those who get testicular cancer: young men, almost all white and predominantly in middle- and upper-middle-class jobs. It was, he joked, very much a disease of young university professors. No researcher understood why testicular cancer had this profile because nothing about the habits, risks, or lifestyle of this group seemed to suggest a connection. But there it was. The worst news was the prognosis. We were told that testicular cancer was one of the most lethal cancers, virtually untreatable, with a life expectancy of about six months. What dying was like was left to our imaginations.

There seems to be an increased risk of testicular cancer among men who had undescended testicles as a child, but beyond this we know nothing about the cause of the disease. However, the visiting professor was wrong, even then, in saying that testicular cancer was untreatable. Today it is one of the most successfully treated forms of cancer, though success varies, depending on how early it is diagnosed.

When I felt that ridge developing on my own testicle, I knew enough to think of cancer but not enough to realize it could be treated. What I remembered from that seminar sounded like a particularly unattractive death sentence, a painful and degrading way to go. Panicked but not totally irrational, I quickly made an appointment with my doctor. He looked somewhat distressed when I told him what was wrong, but he examined me, and to our mutual relief said he felt nothing that might be cancer. The left testicle felt smaller and harder, but nothing suggested a tumor. This was, of course, exactly what I wanted to hear. I was so relieved that I hardly thought to question his diagnosis of chlamydia, a disease that was new to me at that time.

Although easily cured in men, chlamydia is legally quarantinable because it is a leading cause of infertility in women. My doctor told me I might have gotten chlamydia from a public toilet or a hot tub, and did not tell me I had to take precautions against transmitting it sexually. He did not even ask me whether I was married or had sexual partners. Given his lack of advice and the danger chlamydia would have been to my wife, it is fortunate in one sense that his diagnosis was wrong.

But on that day I was only too happy to accept his diagnosis. I could relax; I did not have cancer, and I was not aware of the problems associated with the chlamydia I thought I had. All I had to do was take some penicillin and everything would be fine. Why question a diagnosis that was so much better than the alternative? The answer, of course, is that my life was at stake — but I still retained my old belief that testicular cancer was a death sentence, so I clung to any alternative.

As the first prescription of penicillin ran out and the discomfort turned to pain, I had trouble sustaining my optimism. My doctor prescribed another course of penicillin, telling me that these things take time to clear up. Soon after the testicle soreness began, I had noticed an unfamiliar back pain while running. I had attributed this to the muscular stress of getting back into shape after my heart problems, but now the pain was becoming intense, waking me in the morning. My physician confirmed the muscular nature of the back pain, declared it unrelated to the testicular soreness, and switched my drug prescription to sulfa, saying that sometimes penicillin does not clear up chlamydia. When I had a reaction to the sulfa, he took me off drugs entirely and made an appointment for me to see a urologist — scheduled for two months later.

By early September my condition had deteriorated. The back pains were so severe that I was forced to get up in the middle of the night to relieve the pressure caused by lying on my back. Rest was impossible. One Sunday morning after a sleepless night I was in such pain that I could hardly stand. Since I could expect little more from my usual physician, and it was Sunday, Cathie drove me to the hospital emergency room. When the routine blood and urine tests and X-ray showed nothing abnormal, I was diagnosed as chronically constipated and sent home with the advice to avoid dairy products and eat more fruit. As I remember it, no "hands on" examination was done; the lab tests were presumed to tell all. At that point two physicians were telling me that nothing much was wrong. I wanted to believe them, but my body insisted otherwise.

To quiet my complaints about back pain, my physician sent me to a sports medicine specialist. Nothing irritates me more than politicians' and physicians' complaints about "doctor shopping," or "double doctoring," as an equally insulting phrase has it. If I had not doctor shopped for a *third* opinion, I would probably be dead, because the tumors involved in testicular cancer are among the fastest growing, and the success of treatment varies directly with early detection. Fortunately, the sports medicine specialist I saw was also a skilled internist. He had the good judgment to look beyond muscular-skeletal causes; he actually probed my abdomen with his hands, locating what felt like a mass. When I asked him what he thought this was, he mentioned the possibility of cancer. By then I felt less terrorized by the idea of cancer than validated by a recognition that I was seriously ill.

I had been in too much pain for too long, and I was relieved, at least momentarily, to be told that yes, he believed that something was wrong with me. Being told that you may have cancer does not have to be devastating. Even though my worst fears were realized in what he said, the physician showed, just by the way he looked at me and a couple of phrases he used, that he shared in the seriousness of my situation. The vitality of his support was as personal as it was professional. Physicians I encountered later were optimistic about my diagnosis and prognosis; he was almost alone in expressing optimism about me, not as a case but as a person.

With this third opinion on record, the medical investigation began to move. Several days later I was sent for an ultrasound, a noninvasive test often used for fetal monitoring. I seemed to be the only one in the waiting room who was not pregnant. Ultrasound is exciting for the patient because the physician can tell you what he is finding as he sees the X-ray images on a TV monitor next to you. In my case, however, the diagnosis was a little too exciting.

Here I had half good luck — an excellent technician who was a terrible communicator. This physician told me he observed massive lymphadenopathy, or enlargement of the lymph nodes, behind my stomach. When I asked what would cause this, he abruptly told me it was either a primary or a secondary tumor. Either the nodes were malignant in themselves, or their growth was a development from a malignant tumor elsewhere. Looking back, I respect what that physician was able to discover. But at the time in that basement laboratory, all I could think about was being told I had massive tumors. The physician added nothing to his abrupt statement. He would send a report to my family physician; that was it, not even a goodbye or good luck, just over and out. It was a triumph of science and a lapse of humanity.

When I had left the sports medicine specialist's office I had felt that someone was taking my pain seriously and that a physician could be a source of real support. Walking out of the ultrasound lab, I faced the reality of cancer and felt completely alone. In the weeks before, I had been dealing with pain that made even walking difficult, but now that pain was only numbness.

What was it like to be told I had cancer? The future disappeared. Loved ones became faces I would never see again. I felt I was walking through a nightmare that was unreal but utterly real. This could not be happening to me, but it was, and it would continue to happen. My body had become a kind of quicksand, and I was sinking into myself, my disease.

Just as Cathie and I were putting our lives back together after my heart problems, cancer was ripping us up again, like the street near us that the city seems to dig up every year. As soon as it is paved and traffic is moving, some pipe breaks or some cable needs repair. Up go the roadblocks and in come the jackhammers. Our lives were like that: another year, another disaster.

After an incident like my heart attack I was able to bounce back. People even said, "You've really bounced back." That's accurate, because in most cases we do not sink into an experience, we only hit the surface. I may have bounced back from a heart attack, but with cancer I was going to have to sink all the way through and discover a life on the other side. Cancer was not going to be an incident; I would have to experience it.

Seeing Through Pain

HOW DOCTORS CAME to realize that I had cancer is only the institutional part of the story of becoming ill again. The medical experience has its place, but more important is what I was experiencing in my body. That story begins with pain. Medicine has not conquered pain, though it has developed the means to control pain during much of critical illness. Pain is experienced most at the beginning of illness, before physicians understand what is happening, and at the end, when the body becomes unpredictable. Since my experience happily did not reach that end, pain belongs at the beginning of my story.

Pain is the body's response to illness; it is the first thing many people associate with illness and what they fear most. Whether or not pain is the most difficult part of cancer to live through, it is probably the hardest to describe. We have plenty of words to describe specific pains: sharp, throbbing, piercing, burning, even dull. But these words do not describe the experience of pain. We lack terms to express what it means to live "in" such pain. Unable to express pain, we come to believe there is nothing to say. Silenced, we become isolated in pain, and the isolation increases the pain. Like the sick feeling that comes with the recognition of yourself as ill, there is a pain attached to being in pain.

My pain was the result of pressure exerted by the secondary tumors in my back, a pressure that became more acute when I lay down for some time. In the mornings I would wake up feeling a viselike pressure on my lower back around the kidneys. Soon the pain began to wake me at night, preventing me from sleeping. After several nights I was too tired to shake off sleep entirely, even though rest was impossible. I spent those nights in a kind of limbo between waking and dozing, always inside the pain.

My disease connected pain with night. As the tumors took over my body, pain took over my mind. Darkness compounds the isolation and loneliness of pain, for the sufferers are separated from those whose bodies lie quiet. In darkness the world of those in pain becomes unglued, incoherent.

In writing about the incoherence of pain, one risks becoming incoherent all over again. Language easily goes wrong. I could write that at night in pain I came to know illness face to face. But this metaphor distorts the experience. However much I wanted to give illness a face — to give it any kind of coherence — it is not a presence. Giving illness a face, a temptation enhanced by the dark, only muddles things further. At night I faced only myself.

When we feel ourselves being taken over by something we do not understand, the human response is to create a mythology of what threatens us. We turn pain into "it," a god, an enemy to be fought. We think pain is victimizing us, either because "it" is malevolent or because we have done something to deserve its wrath. We curse it and pray for mercy from it. But pain has no face because it is not alien. It is from myself. Pain is my body signaling that something is wrong. It is the body talking to itself, not the rumblings of an external god. Dealing with pain is not war with something outside the body; it is the body coming back to itself.

But taking pain entirely into my own body, making it too much my own, carries the danger of becoming isolated in that body. Isolation is the beginning of incoherence. When the body is healthy, it coheres, its parts work in concert, and it fits into its environment. Lying down, the body finds comfort and rest. Waking, it is ready for activity. In pain the natural rhythm of rest and activity is lost, and that loss leads to further losses of plans and expectations, of a life that makes sense as a fitting together of past and future. Order breaks down, and incoherence takes its place.

At night, while others are sleeping, it is coherent to sleep, to share that rest. To be summoned out of that rest is an incoherence, a loss of the wholeness that is the natural cycle of life among others. But again my language slips. No thing summoned me from sleep. Bodily pain woke me, and the consciousness of this pain turned into the incoherence of being awake, isolated from those who slept.

Pain is thus one of the first experiences an ill person has of being cast out. To regain a sense of coherence, in which pain may have to remain a part, the ill person has to find a way back in among those he has become separated from.

When I was awake at night in pain, I could have woken

Cathie. I could have called her to witness the pain and to break the loneliness, but waking her would have violated the coherence of her natural cycle of daily life. She still worked during the day and slept at night. Her life retained the coherence mine had lost. I was outside that natural cycle. During the day I was too tired to work, during the night the hammering in my back prevented me from sleeping. I was neither daily nor nocturnal, but suspended outside the limits of either existence. I was neither functionally present nor accountably absent. I lived my life out of place.

I used to have nightmares of finding myself in a place I knew to be forbidden, without any clothes and having to get back (in dreams you never know where) without being seen. Sometimes the nightmare would become an adventure. I would half fly and half flow, silent and naked, through dark, empty alleyways. Other times I would be caught out, fumbling and immobile, for all to see. Part of the fear in such dreams is of being out of place. I was no less out of place on those nights I half sat and half lay, trying to find a position outside of the pain.

I fantasized that this pain was "just for tonight," that it was muscular stress and would be gone tomorrow. This fantasy was fueled by my fear of what might truly be wrong with me, but it was also supported by what my doctor was telling me. One night he prescribed a strong sedative, and when I awoke even from that, the nightmares that accompanied me out of sleep did give incoherence a form and a face. After that night I could no longer sustain my part of what had been my doctor's and my mutual fantasy.

But I have only half-answered the question of why I did not

wake my wife. The other reason is that her sleep was the only coherence left. Although I could no longer share in others' rest, I cared for it all the more. If I could not sleep, I could still love her sleep. Disturbing it would have been the most painful thing I could do. Later, when I was very ill, I watched people out running and loved their capacity for movement, their freedom within their bodies. My hope was that they also valued what they were able to be.

I wish I could finish my story about pain with some formula I learned for dealing with it. But I never learned one. By the time I entered the hospital, the tumors had shifted or somehow changed, allowing me to lie in bed comfortably. There is probably some medical explanation for this change, but it does not interest me much. What counts is that the pain did its proper work: it forced me to get another medical opinion. By the date of the urology appointment made by my family physician, I had already had surgery and one chemotherapy treatment. Pain was the ally it is designed to be, my body's way of insisting that something must change.

Although I never discovered a formula for dealing with pain, I did manage to break through its incoherence one night before it abated. Making my way upstairs, I was stopped on the landing by the sight — the vision really — of a window. Outside the window I saw a tree, and the streetlight just beyond was casting the tree's reflection on the frosted glass. Here suddenly was beauty, found in the middle of a night that seemed to be only darkness and pain. Where we see the face of beauty, we are in our proper place, and all becomes coherent. As I looked at the window it formed a kind of haiku for me:

The streetlight behind the branches
Projects patterns
On a misted window
Do not wipe the glass
Lest others wake.

I realized that if illness has a face, it could be the beauty of that light. But I did not see the face of illness in that window any more than I had seen it in the nightmares caused by pain breaking through the sedative. The window was no myth, no metaphor. It was exactly what it was, and seeing it completely absorbed my attention. I was still in pain, but the pain had brought me to that landing, which was the only place I could be to see the beauty of that window. Coherence was restored.

But coherence does not go without saying; it requires expression. However poor my verse was, I was once again expressing myself. Pain that is inexpressible isolates us; to be mute is to be cast out from others. Whatever form our expression takes, we offer that expression to others, whether or not anyone else is there. Expression implies the presence of others, and we begin again to share in humanity. Others slept their orderly sleep, and I, in my place as they were in theirs, saw something of beauty. I remained alone, but my words put me in the presence of those others.

It is just as hard to write about the coherence I felt as it is to write about incoherence. But it does not matter if my words are not coherent. For the ill person, the attempt to communicate creates an experience of coherence. The particular words in my verse did not matter; it was my attempt at expression that created coherence. I needed the window to see the verse, and I needed the verse to place my seeing in the world of others and thus regain my place in that world.

It is easier to write of caring. I knew that others were sleeping, and I cared for their sleep; I knew there were things of beauty in the night that I cared for. These feelings made pain something I could live with. At the moment when the incoherence of illness and pain makes it seem that all you have lived for has been taken away or is about to be lost, you can find another coherence in which to live. That night the pain mattered less, not because I dissociated myself from my body, but rather because I associated myself beyond my body. Caring for Cathie's sleep or for that window gave me the coherence I needed to go on caring for myself. I had not yet been sick enough to understand all I saw in that window; only later would language catch up to experience. But at least that night I knew I was in a place I could care for.

Mourning What Is Lost

THE LOSS THAT accompanies illness begins in the body, as pain does, then moves out until it affects the relationships connecting that body with others. Those relationships first became strained during the weeks when I was getting bad medical news, but a diagnosis of cancer had not yet been confirmed. My body had lost its predictable capacity to sleep or walk, taking away my ability to make plans and accept responsibilities. But I did not want to believe I had cancer, and others did not want to hear about that possibility. My awkward attempts to avoid commitments I was not sure I could fulfill only made people think I was distancing myself from them. I acted not from lack of friendship but because my body was taking me out of their natural flow of plans and expectations. Others took planning for granted; my future was pervaded by uncertainty. I lost my sense of belonging.

The inability to make specific plans is only the beginning of the loss of belonging. On the day the ultrasound tests showed lymphadenopathy, I made it home in pretty good control of myself. I was alone because my mother-in-law was beginning a new round of chemotherapy that day. Cathie and I had decided, perhaps in a moment of mutual denial of what was happening to me, that she should be with her mother. When I walked back into our house, she was still out, and what had happened crashed down on me. All I could see were faces I would never grow old with — my daughter from my first marriage, Cathie, my parents. I believed I was going to die, much sooner than later. The pain of my death was in losing my future with those others. My reasons for living have never been clearer.

Loss of the future is complemented by loss of the past. I felt this loss most keenly one night shortly before the surgery to remove the tumorous testicle. The surgery is called an orchidectomy or sometimes orchiectomy, from the Greek *orchi,* for testis. The name still reminds me of an exotic flower, which the operation would pluck. I found this amusing. The coming operation did not distress me; I had had too much pain to feel any great attachment to that part of my body. I was told I would have no impairment of sexual functioning from the loss of one testicle. If I had been in my late teens, as some testicular cancer patients are, the operation would have had a different meaning. At my age I was more interested in being able to pull on a pair of pants without wincing.

I did feel I was losing my body's continuity with its youth. Middle age insinuates itself slowly into our bodies and lives. It is the time when on a good day you can still kid yourself into thinking you are as young as ever. Several nights before surgery, I looked at myself in a mirror. The body I saw was not the body I had had at twenty-two or even thirty, but it retained for me a continuity with those bodies. The changes, the deteriorations, had been gradual. On another night I might have been able to kid myself into seeing the thirty-year-old.

That night I knew that after surgery I would never be the same. By then I was aware that chemotherapy could effectively shrink the tumors along my back. Even so, I would not be the same. Surgery and chemotherapy would irrevocably break my body's continuity with its past. I did not dread what I would become, but I needed to mourn the end of what I had been. It was like saying goodbye to a place I had lived in and loved. I had tried to take care of my body, and it had treated me well enough, but now treatments I did not yet understand would change it into something else.

When you say goodbye to your body, as I was doing that night, you say goodbye to how you have lived. An old aphorism says that after a certain age every man is responsible for his own face. Each person records the history of his life on his body. My history had it share of regrets, but I mourned its passing. After surgery and chemotherapy rearranged me, I would live differently. This difference is made up of gains as much as losses, but at that moment the gains were unknowable and the losses were before me in the mirror.

Other losses went beyond the body. Cathie and I had always hoped that if the worst happened, friends and relatives would respond with care and involvement. Then the worst did happen, and we no longer expected what others would do, we knew. Some came through; others disappeared. We now find it hard to resume relationships with those who could not acknowledge the illness that was happening, not just to me but to us. Those relationships were a loss.

Together Cathie and I lost an innocence about the normal expectations of life. At one time it seemed normal to expect to work and accomplish certain things, to have children and watch them grow, to share experiences with others, to grow old together. Now we realize that these events may or may not happen. Life is contingent. We are no longer sure what it is normal to expect. At a later time this loss of innocent expectation can be seen as a gain from illness, but at first it feels like a loss.

These losses of future and past, of place and innocence, whether they are ours together or mine alone, must all be mourned. The ill person's losses vary according to one's life and illness. We should never question what a person chooses to mourn. One person's losses may seem eccentric to another, but the loss is real enough, and that reality deserves to be honored. I was fortunate to have a wife to share my mourning. Sharing losses seemed to be the gentlest way of living with them.

I have written of my own losses and something of ours together, but nothing of the losses that were Cathie's alone. Even now I probably recognize only some of these. The caregiver often has more difficulty finding time and recognition for mourning. While I was ill we knew that she, the caregiver, needed to mourn and recognize losses as much as I, the ill person. We both had to let our grieving run its course. But despite our intentions, this natural sequence did not happen. Before we had time to mourn the experience of my illness, Cathie's mother became critically ill and eventually died. During her illness the levels of mourning were compounded, and we had to place our earlier mourning on hold. Through these experiences we learned how the failure to mourn impairs a life.

Most people's problems with mourning are not caused by compounded losses; their problems are caused by other people's desires to get mourning over with. Medical staff, family, and friends all want the ill person or caregiver to accommodate to loss, whether it is caused by illness or by death, as quickly as possible. Mourning slows down the treatment of the ill and reminds others of their own mortality. Society pressures us to return to the healthy mainstream, minimizing and forgetting our losses.

Professionals talk too much about adjustment. I want to emphasize mourning as affirmation. To mourn what has passed, either through illness or death, affirms the life that has been led. To adjust too rapidly is to treat the loss as simply an incident from which one can bounce back; it devalues whom or what has been lost. When an ill person loses the body in which she has lived, or when a caregiver suffers the death of the person he has cared for, the loss must be mourned fully and in its own time. Only through that mourning can we find a life on the other side of loss.

I suggested that this book is in some sense a series of letters to my younger self before I became ill. I want to tell that self to let yourself grieve your losses and to find people who will accept that grieving. Avoid those who seek to minimize what you have lost, whether by comparing your losses to those of others or by telling you you'll soon get used to it. The losses you go through are real, and no one should take these away from you. They are a part of your experience, and you are entitled to them. Illness can teach that every part of life is worth experiencing, even the losses. To grieve well is to value what you have lost. When you value even the feeling of loss, you value life itself, and you begin to live again.

Care Has No Recipe

THE ORDER of the previous chapters may suggest that the experience of illness follows a sequence: first pain, then loss, and so on. Writing creates an illusion of order, but in life experiences overlap. More important, what happened to me was mine alone. The value of telling one particular story in detail is that it shows how unique each of us is. I do not want to generalize my experience of illness into some set of stages. Only by recognizing the differences in our experiences can we begin to care for each other.

My experiences with heart attack and cancer taught me how different illnesses can be. The first difference is in our fears. With heart problems my fears were of sudden disappearance. But at least as I imagined it, I would have gone out like the athlete dying young in the poem of that title. In full flower, as I thought of it. Thirty-nine is not that young, and I was never much of an athlete, but in imagining my own death I allowed myself some poetic license.

With most cancers there is little fear of sudden death. When I went to sleep I was sure I would wake up in the morning. The problem with cancer is, wake up to what? My fear was less of being dead than of dying slowly, of decaying, suffering interminably, the body spewing out foul fluids. I have now been with enough people dying of cancer to know that their deaths involve fewer of the gruesome details than I feared. Popular fears of cancer, which I shared, exaggerate the drama of its terrors but underestimate the mundane discomforts that accumulate. If a heart attack blows you away, cancer chips at you bit by bit.

Fears vary. Differences in fears are part of the individual experience of illness, and care is about recognizing difference. Care must also recognize how differently people may experience the same disease. How people learn that they have cancer makes a lasting difference. I discovered cancer through pain. One day, before I was diagnosed, I was trying to walk from our home to the university where I teach. It's an easy walk, and I enjoy it. Walking clears my mind. But this day I felt like a balloon was being blown up inside my rib cage, constricting me. I was suffocating from within; stopping did not relieve the pressure. As I got to campus I passed a colleague and found I could not speak to him. I just could not make any words form.

Having that experience prepared me for the medical diagnosis and treatment that came later. Before I called it cancer, I already knew how serious the condition of my body was. I never want to repeat that suffocating, painful experience, but I appreciate having had it. The pain made what was happening to my body real. Other people are told that they have cancer before they have experienced it in their bodies. They find it difficult to know cancer as more than an abstraction.

Six years after her initial diagnosis of cancer, my mother-in-law remarked that she had never suffered from cancer itself. She suffered from medical interventions, but the success of these treatments prevented her from being aware of the disease's effect on her body. Once she bent over to pick up a pencil and felt a sharp pain from compression. She was both frightened and excited when her doctor told her she might have felt the tumors. It was the first time she actually experienced the disease they were treating. I am grateful she did not suffer more, but I think that for her cancer was mostly an abstraction. Cancer was something physicians talked about, and treatment was something they did to her. I think her illness was made more difficult by not having a sense of the disease in her body until near the end, but I doubt that one person can judge another's experience. I claim only that we came to know our illnesses in very different ways.

Another friend remembered the indignation she felt when a physician told her that "cancer was coursing through her body." His comment was devastating to her, but at times I would have found it validating. Whatever was happening in her body, what she was feeling was a tiny lump in her breast. My body was telling me that something awful *was* coursing through it — not a bad description. When I was hardly able to walk, but my family doctor was telling me simply to quit running and see a urologist in a couple of months, it was reassuring to have other physicians acknowledge that the problems were as real as I felt they were.

When I was finally told how sick I was, the essential difference between the diagnoses by the sports medicine specialist and the ultrasound physician was in the support each gave me. The two diagnoses were about the same, but the sports medicine physician involved himself in what he was telling me, while the other physician pronounced his diagnosis like a verdict. Differences proliferate: the same message can have different meanings for different ill persons, and the same content can become two different messages, depending on how it is delivered.

Care begins when difference is recognized. There is no "right thing to say to a cancer patient," because the "cancer patient" as a generic entity does not exist. There are only persons who are different to start with, having different experiences according to the contingencies of their diseases. The common diagnostic categories into which medicine places its patients are relevant to disease, not to illness. They are useful for treatment, but they only get in the way of care.

Most people who deal with ill persons do not want to recognize differences and particularities because sorting them out requires time. Even to learn what the differences are, you have to become involved. Generalities save time. Placing people in categories, the fewer the better, is efficient; each category indicates a common treatment: one size fits all. But again, treatment is not care. Treatment gets away with making a compromise between efficiency and care by creating an illusion of involvement. This illusion often begins with a recipe, made up of key words referring to psychological states, that tells treatment providers what behavior to expect.

The most famous recipe is Elisabeth Kübler-Ross's stage theory of the experience of dying: the dying person goes through denial, anger, bargaining, grief, and acceptance. Although I do not think it was Kübler-Ross's original intent, her theory has been used to categorize rather than to open up

people's experiences. Instead of guiding us into what is particular about an individual's experiences with illness, these
words create distance, allowing others to say, "As we expected, he's going through anger." Rather than asking why
the ill person is angry, anger becomes "just a stage." And since
we expected it, we can dismiss it as "something everyone goes
through."

What makes an experience real is its particulars. One person's anger or grief may differ so much from another's that
calling them by a common name only obscures what is actually going on for each. The word — anger, grief, or whatever — conceals more than it reveals. The popularity of such
a theory is not surprising. Persons using such words think they
can understand without having to become involved in the
texture of lived experience with all its variations. They can
even draw others into this illusion of understanding.

Stage theories can be valuable for ill persons, however, if
not for caregivers. Those who are ill find it valuable to know
that others share their experiences. When I was panicked
by the diagnosis of cancer, I took comfort from knowing
that panic is a "normal" reaction upon hearing a diagnosis
of life-threatening disease. When I felt disoriented and depressed, I knew I wasn't going crazy; this too is normal.
Knowing that others go through these experiences made my
own panic, disorientation, and depression feel less personal,
less specific to me. But the caregiver must remember that my
panic *is* mine entirely, not some "stage." The last thing an ill
person needs is to be treated as "only going through the panic
stage." The individual's panic may be mitigated because it is
shared, but it cannot be dismissed because it is expected.

Knowing that panic is normal does not resolve the feelings evoked in that panic.

After persons receive a diagnosis of serious illness, the support they need varies as widely as humanity itself. Some want to have family gathered around them, others need to be alone. Some need the assurance of immediate medical intervention, others have to have some time to decide what treatment they want. A physician may help one person by rushing in, another, by backing off. The caregiver's art is finding a way to allow the ill person to express his needs. Eventually a balance must be worked out between what the ill person needs and what the caregivers are able to provide. In order to find that balance, caregivers, whether professional, family, or friends, must help the ill person figure out what he needs. Only then can they negotiate what they are prepared to provide.

It takes time for an ill person to understand her needs. The caregiver cannot simply ask "What do you need?" and expect a coherent reply. A recently diagnosed person's life has already changed in more ways than she can grasp, and changes continue throughout critical illness. Part of what is "critical" is the persistence of change. Being critically ill means never being able to keep up with your own needs. Except for the need to hear that it is all a mistake — the lab results had the wrong name on them; I'm fine, really — the ill person does not know what she needs, though the needs are very real.

The day I had the ultrasound, which strongly suggested that I had cancer, a visiting professor happened to be in town to act as external examiner for a Ph.D. candidate in my department. Cathie and I were supposed to take him to dinner that night. After the ultrasound she and I had some time to go through various emotions together. We acknowledged that what we each had feared was now real, we cursed the medical system for being so slow, and we tried to be optimistic about the physician I was now being sent to. We found ways to let each other know that our love carried on. Then we picked up our guest and went to dinner, with no mention of cancer.

His company was the perfect vehicle for the denial we needed that night. Being out with him put cancer on hold for awhile, and during that time we realized that there could still be pleasant evenings; life would go on, even with cancer. We could never have planned what happened, but we were able to use it to meet our needs. Perhaps you should not even try to put your needs into words. All you can do is let yourself discover these needs, and all others can do is give you the time and space to make this discovery.

I reserve the name "caregivers" for the people who are willing to listen to ill persons and to respond to their individual experiences. Caring has nothing to do with categories; it shows the person that her life is valued because it recognizes what makes her experience particular. One person has no right to categorize another, but we do have the privilege of coming to understand how each of us is unique. When the caregiver communicates to the ill person that she cares about that uniqueness, she makes the person's life meaningful. And as that person's life story becomes part of her own, the caregiver's life is made meaningful as well. Care is inseparable from understanding, and like understanding, it must be symmetrical. Listening to another, we hear ourselves. Caring for another, we either care for ourselves as well, or we end in burnout and frustration.

Most medical staff do not have the time to be caregivers, and many may not have the inclination. They provide treatment, which is no less important than caregiving, but it is not at all the same. Too often even the family members who remain involved with the ill person rather than defecting also become service providers rather than caregivers.

Caregivers are confronted not with an ordered sequence of illness experiences, but with a stew of panic, uncertainty, fear, denial, and disorientation, with bargaining quickly added. Cathie had to listen for days to my bargaining one diagnostic or treatment possibility against another. "I'll suffer this if I don't have to have that." It takes the ill person some time to realize there is nothing and no one to bargain with. Loneliness also enters, then doubts about who you are and what your life is worth, hope mixed with depression, anger mixed with a desire for contact with others, dependency mixed with a need to continue to do things for yourself.

What I have just written only suggests the stew of an ill person's feelings, but even that returns me to my central point: none of these words mean anything. Terms like pain or loss have no reality until they are filled in with an ill person's own experience. Witnessing the particulars of that experience, and recognizing all its differences, is care.

The Body as Territory
and as Wonder

I HAVE PUT my body in the hands of physicians off and on since the day I was born. But until I was critically ill I never felt I was putting my life in their hands. Life-threatening illness gave doctors a new dimension of importance for me. I had never expected so much from them or been so sensitive to their shortcomings. How medicine treats the body is an essential part of the story of illness, but it is never more than half of the story. The other half is the body itself. Life-threatening illness also gave my body a new dimension of importance. I had never been so sensitive to its shortcomings, nor had I realized how much I could expect of it. These two stories, the story of medicine taking the body as its territory and the story of learning to wonder at the body itself, can only be told to-gether, because illness is both stories at once.

After the ultrasound a physician said, "This will have to be investigated." Hearing this phrase, I was both relieved and offended. The relief was that someone was assuming part of the burden of worrying about what was happening to me. But

I was also offended by his language, which made my body into medicine's field of investigation. "I" had become medicine's "this." The physician did not even say, "We'll have to find out what's wrong with you," which would have been a team of real people ("we") speaking to another person ("you"). "This will have to be investigated" was not addressed to me at all. The physician was speaking as if to himself, allowing me, the patient, to overhear.

"This will have to be investigated" assumes that physicians will do the investigation, but they too are left out of the phrase, anonymous. "Will have to be" suggests the investigation happens of its own necessity. Why should a physician speak this way? Because if in the course of this investigation mistakes are made (as the physician who spoke had already mistaken my diagnosis), no individual physician is responsible. The mistakes are just part of a process; they too "have to be." I imagine he spoke out of fear as well as uncertainty. He responded by making himself and other physicians anonymous. And I had to be made equally anonymous.

I, my body, became the passive object of this necessity, the investigation. I could imagine how native people felt when European explorers arrived on their shores, planted a flag, and claimed their land on behalf of a foreign monarch who would bring civilization to the savages. To get medicine's help, I had to cede the territory of my body to the investigation of doctors who were as yet anonymous. I had to be colonized.

The investigation required me to enter the hospital. Fluids were extracted, specialists' opinions accumulated, machines produced images of the insides of my body, but the diagnosis remained uncertain. One day I returned to my room and found a new sign below my name on the door. It said "Lymphoma," a form of cancer I was suspected of having. No one had told me that this diagnosis, which later proved to be wrong, had been confirmed. Finding it written there was like the joke about the guy who learns he has been fired when he finds someone else's name on his office door. In this case my name had not been changed, it had been defined. "Lymphoma" was a medical flag, planted as a claim on the territory of my body.

This colonization only became worse. During chemotherapy a nurse, speaking to Cathie, referred to me as "the seminoma in 53" (my room number). By then the diagnosis was correct, but it had crowded out my name entirely. The hospital had created its own version of my identity. I became the disease, the passive object of investigation and later of treatment. Nameless, how could I be a person who experiences?

The ill person actively tries to make sense of what is happening in her body. She tries to maintain a relationship between what is happening to her body and what is going on in the rest of her life. When a person becomes a patient, physicians take over her body, and their understanding of the body separates it from the rest of her life. Medicine's understanding of pain, for instance, has little to do with the ill person's experience. For the person, pain is about incoherence and the disruption of relations with other people and things; it is about losing one sense of place and finding another. Medicine has no interest in what pain means in a life; it can see pain only as a symptom of a possible disease. Medicine cannot enter into the experience; it seeks only cure or management. It does offer relief to a body that is suffering, but in doing so it colonizes the body. This is the trade-off we make in seeking medical help.

If the treatment works, the passivity is worth it. When I am ill, I want to become a patient. It is dangerous to avoid doctors, but it is equally dangerous to allow them to hog center stage in the drama of illness. The danger of avoiding doctors is immediate and physical, but if we allow them to dominate the drama, they will script it to include only disease. By saying "This will have to be investigated," my physician claimed center stage and scripted the drama to follow; the person within my body was sent out into the audience to watch passively.

What did I, as patient, want from physicians and the medical staff? I did not expect to become friends with them. In the hospital I had such fleeting contact with so many specialists, and nurses appeared to rotate through shifts so rapidly, that exchanging anything more than conventional pleasantries would have been artificial. The relationship of patient to staff is peculiar, unlike any other. We discussed intimate matters, but this talk did not make us close. As treatment providers, they saw my intimate concerns in the context of their general categories of disease and the progress of treatment.

Relationships between patients and medical staff, whether physicians or nurses, involve people who are intimate with each other but rarely become intimates of each other. For a truly intimate relationship people need a sharing of time and personal history and a recognition of each other's differences. Medical intimacy categorizes rather than recognizes, and it is one-sided. The patient's life and body are an open book, or chart, to the medical staff. The staff sometimes share their experiences with patients, but in my memory these moments are the exceptions. More important, physicians and nurses can choose what they will tell a patient about themselves, and whether they will say anything at all. There is the real asymmetry, which becomes more complicated during moments that are critical in the patient's life but represent just another day's work for the staff. The staff cannot match the patient's emotional intensity on such occasions, but they should not expect the patient to mimic their professional calm.

I may not expect emotion or intimacy from physicians and nurses, but I do expect recognition. Another person, whose experience I want to honor, said it is no small thing to have cancer — to realize you are becoming ill, to suffer that illness and risk death, to be dying or to have returned to the living and be starting life over again with the knowledge of your own mortality. It is no small thing to have your body rearranged, first by disease and then by surgical and chemical interventions intended to cure that disease. Critical illness takes its travelers to the margins of human experience. One step further and someone so ill would not return. I want that journey to be recognized.

I always assumed that if I became seriously ill, physicians, no matter how overworked, would somehow recognize what I was living through. I did not know what form this recognition would take, but I assumed it would happen. What I experienced was the opposite. The more critical my diagnosis became, the more reluctant physicians were to talk to me. I had trouble getting them to make eye contact; most came only to see my disease. This "it" within the body was their field of investigation; "I" seemed to exist beyond the horizon of their interest.

Medical staff often believe they are involved in the patient's personal life. When I was admitted to the hospital, the resident doing my intake physical made a point of saying he was now getting to the "social history." Cathie and I were curious to know what the hospital considered important as social history. The resident then asked what my job was. I answered and waited for the next question; he closed the chart. That was it, nothing more. What bothered us was the illusion that he had found out something. The resident took his inquiry into my social history seriously and seemed to have no sense of how little he learned. The irony of there being only one question completely escaped him. He was filling in a category, employment, to give himself an illusion of having recognized me as a "social" being.

The night before I had surgery, I was visited by an anesthesiologist who represented the culmination of my annoyance with this nonrecognition. He refused to look at me, and he even had the facts of the planned operation wrong. When he was leaving I did the worst thing to him I could think of: I made him shake hands. A hand held out to be shaken cannot be refused without direct insult, but to shake a hand is to acknowledge the other as an equal. The anesthesiologist trembled visibly as he brushed his hand over mine, and I allowed myself to enjoy his discomfort. But that was only a token of what I really wanted. I wanted him to recognize that the operation I was having and the disease it was part of were no small thing.

The kind of recognition I wanted changed over the course of my illness. While seeking diagnosis I felt that I was in a struggle just to get physicians to recognize the disease; once I got them onto the stage of my illness, the problem was to keep it my drama, not theirs. The active roles in the drama of illness all go to physicians. Being a patient means, quite literally, being patient. Daily life in the hospital is spent waiting for physicians. Hospitals are organized so that physicians can see a maximum number of patients, which means patients spend maximum time waiting. You have to be patient. Maybe the doctor will come this morning; if not, maybe this afternoon. Decisions about treatment are stalled until the doctor's arrival; nurses and residents don't know what's happening. Hopes, fears, and uncertainty mount.

When the physician does arrive, he commands center stage. I write "he" because this performance is so stereotypically masculine, although women physicians learn to play it well enough. The patient hangs on what brief words are said, what parts of the body are examined or left unattended. When the physician has gone, the patient recounts to visitors everything he did and said, and together they repeatedly consider and interpret his visit. The patient wonders what the physician meant by this joke or that frown. In hospitals, where the patient is constantly reminded of how little he knows, the physician is assumed not only to know all but to know more than he says.

In becoming a patient — being colonized as medical territory and becoming a spectator to your own drama — you lose yourself. First you may find that the lab results rather than your body's responses are determining how you feel. Then, in the rush to treatment, you may lose your capacity to make choices, to decide how you want your body to be used. Finally, in the blandness of the medical setting, in its routines and their discipline, you may forget your tastes and preferences. Life turns to beige. It is difficult to accept the realities of what physicians can do for you without subordinating yourself to their power. The power is real, but it need not be total. You can find places for yourself in the cracks.

I want to affirm the importance, both for yourself and for those around you, of holding onto the person you still are, even as medicine tries to colonize your body. Disease cannot be separated from other parts of a person's identity and life. Disease changed my life as husband, father, professor, and everything else. I had to learn to be dependent. I was unreliable in practical matters and often in emotional ones as well, and incapable of doing tasks that I had considered normal. It was no small thing to rediscover myself as I changed.

I have learned that the changes that begin during illness do not end when treatment stops. Life after critical illness does not go back to where it was before. A danger of allowing physicians to dominate the drama of illness is that they leave as soon as the disease is resolved to their satisfaction or when they have done all they can. Then the ill person and those around him are left to deal with the consequences of what has not been recognized. If the ill person dies, those who survive must deal with all that was not said, the unfinished business of a life closed out in a setting where dying is a problem of management, not a continuity of experience. And those ill persons who recover must recover not only from the disease but from being a patient. This recovery will proceed far more smoothly if the person within the patient has been recognized throughout the period of illness and recovery.

Continuing to recognize myself as the person undergoing

the illness, reclaiming my body as my territory while I was in settings dominated by what was relevant to medicine alone, was no easy business.

What authorizes medicine to claim the body as its territory? Every day society sends us messages that the body can and ought to be controlled. Advertisements for prescription and nonprescription drugs, grooming and beauty advice, diet books, and fitness promotion literature all presuppose an ideal of control of the body. Control is good manners as well as a moral duty; to lose control is to fail socially and morally. But then along comes illness, and the body goes out of control.

In society's view of disease, when the body goes out of control, the patient is treated as if he has lost control. Being sick thus carries more than a hint of moral failure; I felt that in being ill I was being vaguely irresponsible. Of course, the problem is not that I or any other ill person has "lost" control; the problem is that society's ideal of controlling the body is wrong in the first place. But rather than give up this ideal, society sends in physicians to prove that bodies can be controlled. Physicians justifiably think it is their duty to restore, in the name of society, the control that the sick are believed to have lost. Control, or at least management, becomes a medical ideal.

A cousin who had cancer wrote to me about a meeting she had with her doctor in which she asked more questions than he apparently thought appropriate. He accused her of "trying to control" her treatment, and asserted that he was "in control." This story is not uncommon, though it seems to happen more often to women patients than to men. The real question is not who is in control, but whether anyone is. One lesson I have learned from illness is that giving up the idea of control, by either myself or my doctors, made me more content. What I recommend, to both medical staff and ill persons, is to recognize the wonder of the body rather than try to control it.

Wondering at the body means trusting it and acknowledging its control. I do not mean that we should stop trying to change the direction the body is taking. I certainly did all I could, and I value all that my physicians did, to use treatment to change the direction my body was taking. Wonder and treatment can be complementary; wonder is an attitude in which treatment can best proceed. To think that any of us was controlling the body through treatment is another illusion. That my body responded to medical interventions did not mean it was being "successfully" controlled. Rather we should wonder at what "it" did. I use the word "it" here because the body worth wondering at is not the creature of my conscious mind. It is not an extension of "I." Instead, my mind is an extension of my body. I claim little credit for the wonder of my body.

Wonder is almost always possible; control may not be. If the ill person can focus on an ideal of wonder in place of control, then living in a diseased body can recover some of its joy. I did not think this up; I learned it from my body one morning in the rain.

While my investigation was still in the outpatient stage, I used to walk to the hospital for diagnostic tests. One morning I was scheduled to have a pyelogram, a kind of X-ray to test kidney functioning. Cathie was teaching and needed the car. It was pouring rain, coming down in buckets. Any sane person would have called a taxi, but I had cancer and no aspirations to sanity. I wanted to walk. Preparation for the pyelogram required taking massive laxatives to empty the intestine, so in addition to my sleeping problems, I had spent the night in the bathroom.

But as wrecked as I was, when I started walking I began to feel better. I was outside and moving and really very happy. First my feet began to get wet, then my pants, and soon the water was dripping inside my jacket, but that didn't matter. Here was the world of people going to work, of puddles and grass and leaves, and I was able to be part of it. Getting wet was the least of my problems. My problem was going into the hospital, or, more specifically, not coming out again. I feared that the pyelogram's results would mean I couldn't leave the hospital; soon the world I was walking through would be closed off to me. Not today probably; I half realized that before any results were available and medical judgment took over, I would have escaped. But I did not know how many more walks I might have. So I did not lapse into thinking about what I was going to do once I got where I was going; that day I experienced the trip. And I realized that I owed it to illness to be able to see that green September day so very clearly.

I did not want to arrive at the hospital, yet I knew I couldn't slosh around outside much longer. For the first time since the ultrasound several days before, I felt pleasantly relaxed about whatever was to happen. Going inside out of the rain, I wondered at what the body could still do for me, as diseased as I knew it must be. That day I stopped resenting "it" for the pain I had felt and began to appreciate my body, in some ways for the first time in my life. I stopped evaluating my body and began to draw strength from it. And I recognized that this body was me.

Later, when I was admitted to the hospital, the strange progress of my disease had relieved most of the pain, and I started exercising again. Exercising in a hospital is not easy. In Canadian hospitals one gets a private room only by the luck of the moment of arrival or by having some very infectious disease. I was lucky in my timing. I took advantage of my privacy to lift weights Cathie brought for me. Nurses would come in to record my vital signs and find I was out running up and down stairs. Their tolerance was more remarkable than my eccentricity.

Running on the stairs, experiencing the strength I still had, gave me a feeling that my body was doing what it wanted. Through exercise I began to discover what I wanted. Exercise was a way of keeping myself at center stage of my illness. When I had surgery, these activities had to end, but they got me through the period of finding "Lymphoma" written under my name. The hospital had its labels for me, but I could hold onto my identity, which was still rooted in my body, tumorous or not.

Exercising was also a way of telling myself that I would come back from cancer, that my body was still worth taking care of. This affirmation was not, however, a deal. I did not think exercise was part of any cure. It was the way I wanted to live out my life with illness, a way to keep living the life I had, regardless of the progress of disease. Exercise was my expression of wonder at the body.

The arts of being ill and of practicing medicine should

converge in mutual wonder at the body. A physician who does not have this sense of wonder seeks only to cure diseases. Sometimes he succeeds, but if cure is the only objective, not achieving it means he has failed. For the artful physician, wonder precludes failure. The physician and the ill person enter into a relationship of joint wonder at the body, in which failure is as irrelevant as control. The ill person who finds a physician to join in this wonder is fortunate. The body is not a territory to be controlled by either the physician's treatment or the patient's will. Those patients whose physicians remain rooted in disease and cure have to accept medical treatment for what it is, and learn to wonder alone or with other caregivers.

I hope that what I call wonder at the body will not be confused with the particular ways I used my body. It happened that I learned about my body by walking to the hospital and by exercising while I was a patient there, but these activities were not essential to continuing the process of wonder. After surgery I did not have many choices for using my body, and chemotherapy gave me even fewer, since by then I could not read. But I found other sources of coherence, particularly in music. At night when I put my head into a Walkman and listened to Bach, I could forget the implications of being in a hospital. Orchestral music was too busy when heard through my cheap headphones, but Glenn Gould playing the Goldberg Variations brought me a peace and identity my environment could not provide. Only later did I learn that Bach wrote the variations for an insomniac prince.

Listening to that music became an activity for my body. I love running most when moving is pervaded by a sense of rhythm, and listening to Bach's music gave me a sensation of movement. The origins of music are inseparable from dance, and dance is one of the great metaphors of life itself. Until I was ill I had never heard so clearly the dance in the music, and life in the dance. Illness taught me that beyond anything I can do, the body simply is. In the wisdom of my body's being I find myself, over and over again.

The Cost of Appearances

SOCIETY PRAISES ill persons with words such as *courageous, optimistic,* and *cheerful.* Family and friends speak approvingly of the patient who jokes or just smiles, making them, the visitors, feel good. Everyone around the ill person becomes committed to the idea that recovery is the only outcome worth thinking about. No matter what the actual odds, an attitude of "You're going to be fine" dominates the sickroom. Everyone works to sustain it. But how much work does the ill person have to do to make others feel good?

Two kinds of emotional work are involved in being ill. The kind I have written about in earlier chapters takes place when the ill person, alone or with true caregivers, works with the emotions of fear, frustration, and loss and tries to find some coherence about what it means to be ill. The other kind is the work the ill person does to keep up an appearance. This appearance is the expectation that a society of healthy friends, coworkers, medical staff, and others places on an ill person.

The appearance most praised is "I'd hardly have known she was sick." At home the ill person must appear to be engaged in normal family routines; in the hospital she should appear to be just resting. When the ill person can no longer conceal the effects of illness, she is expected to convince others that being ill isn't that bad. The minimal acceptable behavior is praised, faintly, as "stoical." But the ill person may not feel like acting good-humored and positive; much of the time it takes hard work to hold this appearance in place.

I have never heard an ill person praised for how well she expressed fear or grief or was openly sad. On the contrary, ill persons feel a need to apologize if they show any emotions other than laughter. Occasional tears may be passed off as the ill person's need to "let go"; the tears are categorized as temporary outbursts instead of understood as part of an ongoing emotion. Sustained "negative" emotions are out of place. If a patient shows too much sadness, he must be depressed, and "depression" is a treatable medical disease.

Too few people, whether medical staff, family, or friends, seem willing to accept the possibility that depression may be the ill person's most appropriate response to the situation. I am not recommending depression, but I do want to suggest that at some moments even fairly deep depression must be accepted as part of the experience of illness.

A couple of days before my mother-in-law died, she shared a room with a woman who was also being treated for cancer. My mother-in-law was this woman's second dying roommate, and the woman was seriously ill herself. I have no doubt that her diagnosis of clinical depression was accurate. The issue is how the medical staff responded to her depression. Instead of trying to understand it as a reasonable response to her situation, her doctors treated her with antidepressant drugs.

When a hospital psychologist came to visit her, his questions were designed only to evaluate her "mental status." What day is it? Where are you and what floor are you on? Who is Prime Minister? and so forth. His sole interest was whether the dosage of antidepressant drug was too high, upsetting her "cognitive orientation." The hospital needed her to be mentally competent so she would remain a "good patient" requiring little extra care; it did not need her emotions. No one attempted to explore her fears with her. No one asked what it was like to have two roommates die within a couple of days of each other, and how this affected her own fear of death. No one was willing to witness her experience.

What makes me saddest is seeing the work ill persons do to sustain this "cheerful patient" image. A close friend of ours, dying of cancer, seriously wondered how her condition could be getting worse, since she had brought homemade cookies to the treatment center whenever she had chemotherapy. She believed there had to be a causal connection between attitude and physical improvement. From early childhood on we are taught that attitude and effort count. "Good citizenship" is supposed to bring us extra points. The nurses all said what a wonderful woman our friend was. She was the perfectly brave, positive, cheerful cancer patient. To me she was most wonderful at the end, when she grieved her illness openly, dropped her act, and clearly demonstrated her anger. She lived her illness as she chose, and by the time she was acting on her anger and sadness, she was too sick for me to ask her if she wished she had expressed more of those emotions earlier. I can only wonder what it had cost her to sustain her happy image for so long.

When I tried to sustain a cheerful and tidy image, it cost me energy, which was scarce. It also cost me opportunities to express what *was* happening in my life with cancer and to understand that life. Finally, my attempts at a positive image diminished my relationships with others by preventing them from sharing my experience. But this image is all that many of those around an ill person are willing to see.

The other side of sustaining a "positive" image is denying that illness can end in death. Medical staff argue that patients who need to deny dying should be allowed to do so. The sad end of this process comes when the person is dying but has become too sick to express what he might now want to say to his loved ones, about his life and theirs. Then that person and his family are denied a final experience together; not all will choose this moment, but all have a right to it.

The medical staff do not have to be part of the tragedy of living with what was left unsaid. For them a patient who denies is one who is cheerful, makes few demands, and asks fewer questions. Some ill persons may need to deny, for reasons we cannot know. But it is too convenient for treatment providers to assume that the denial comes entirely from the patient, because this allows them not to recognize that they are cueing the patient. Labeling the ill person's behavior as denial describes it as a need of the patient, instead of understanding it as the patient's *response* to his situation. That situation, made up of the cues given by treatment providers and caregivers, is what shapes the ill person's behavior.

To be ill is to be dependent on medical staff, family, and friends. Since all these people value cheerfulness, the ill must summon up their energies to be cheerful. Denial may not be what they want or need, but it is what they perceive those around them wanting and needing. This is not the ill person's own denial, but rather his accommodation to the denial of others. When others around you are denying what is happening to you, denying it yourself can seem like your best deal.

To live among others is to make deals. We have to decide what support we need and what we must give others to get that support. Then we make our "best deal" of behavior to get what we need. This process is rarely a conscious one. It develops over a long time in so many experiences that it becomes the way we are, or what we call our personality. But behind much of what we call personality, deals are being made. In a crisis such as illness the terms of the deal rise to the surface and can be seen more clearly.

One incident can stand for all the deals I made during treatment. During my chemotherapy I had to spend three-day periods as an inpatient, receiving continuous drugs. In the three weeks or so between treatments I was examined weekly in the day-care part of the cancer center. Day care is a large room filled with easy chairs where patients sit while they are given briefer intravenous chemotherapy than mine. There are also beds, closely spaced with curtains between. Everyone can see everyone else and hear most of what is being said. Hospitals, however, depend on a myth of privacy. As soon as a curtain is pulled, that space is defined as private, and the patient is expected to answer all questions, no matter how intimate. The first time we went to day care, a young nurse interviewed Cathie and me to assess our "psychosocial" needs. In the middle of this medical bus station she began asking some reasonable questions. Were we experiencing difficulties at work because of my illness? Were we having any problems with our families? Were we getting support from them? These questions were precisely what a caregiver should ask. The problem was where they were being asked.

Our response to most of these questions was to lie. Without even looking at each other, we both understood that whatever problems we were having, we were not going to talk about them there. Why? To figure out our best deal, we had to assess the kind of support we thought we could get in that setting from that nurse. Nothing she did convinced us that what she could offer was equal to what we would risk by telling her the truth.

Admitting that you have problems makes you vulnerable, but it is also the only way to get help. Throughout my illness Cathie and I constantly weighed our need for help against the risk involved in making ourselves vulnerable. If we did not feel that support was forthcoming, we suppressed our need for expression. If we had expressed our problems and emotions in that very public setting, we would have been extremely vulnerable. If we had then received anything less than total support, it would have been devastating. The nurse showed no awareness or appreciation of how much her questions required us to risk, so we gave only a cheerful "no problems" response. That was all the setting seemed able to support.

Maybe we were wrong. Maybe the staff would have supported us if we had opened up our problems with others' responses to my illness, our stress trying to keep our jobs going, and our fears and doubts about treatment. We certainly were aware that our responses cut off that support. It was double or nothing; we chose safety. Ill persons face such choices constantly. We still believe we were right to keep quiet. If the staff had had real support to offer, they would have offered it in a setting that encouraged our response. When we were alone with nurses in an inpatient room, the questions they asked were those on medical history forms. In the privacy of that room the nurses were vulnerable to the emotions we might have expressed, so they asked no "psychosocial" questions.

It was a lot of work for us to answer the day-care nurse's questions with a smile. Giving her the impression that we felt all right was draining, and illness and its care had drained us both already. But expending our energies this way seemed our best deal.

Anybody who wants to be a caregiver, particularly a professional, must not only have real support to offer but must also learn to convince the ill person that this support is there. My defenses have never been stronger than they were when I was ill. I have never watched others more closely or been more guarded around them. I needed others more than I ever have, and I was also most vulnerable to them. The behavior I worked to let others see was my most conservative estimate of what I thought they would support.

Again I can give no formula, only questions. To the ill person: How much is this best deal costing you in terms of emotional work? What are you compromising of your own expression of illness in order to present those around you with the cheerful appearance they want? What do you fear will happen if you act otherwise? And to those around the ill person: What cues are you giving the ill person that tell her how you want her to act? In what way is her behavior a response to your own? Whose denial, whose needs?

Fear and depression are a part of life. In illness there are no "negative emotions," only experiences that have to be lived through. What is needed in these moments is not denial but recognition. The ill person's suffering should be affirmed, whether or not it can be treated. What I wanted when I was most ill was the response, "Yes, we see your pain; we accept your fear." I needed others to recognize not only that I was suffering, but also that we had this suffering in common. I can accept that doctors and nurses sometimes fail to provide the correct treatment. But I cannot accept it when medical staff, family, and friends fail to recognize that they are equal participants in the process of illness. Their actions shape the behavior of the ill person, and their bodies share the potential of illness.

Those who make cheerfulness and bravery the price they require for support deny their own humanity. They deny that to be human is to be mortal, to become ill and die. Ill persons need others to share in recognizing with them the frailty of the human body. When others join the ill person in this recognition, courage and cheer may be the result, not as an appearance to be worked at, but as a spontaneous expression of a common emotion.

Chemotherapy and Adventure

GOING INTO chemotherapy, I had every hope and just as many fears. Chemotherapy is effective for testicular cancer patients about 80 percent of the time, depending on how far the cancer has progressed. Given the delays in my diagnosis, my odds were probably not that good. But no matter how good or bad the odds were, they were only odds. Getting testicular cancer in the first place did not make me feel lucky. Thus medicine's attitude of "You've got it made" became irritating. I restrained myself from asking physicians or nurses how they would feel if told they had a 20 percent chance of not making it home safe that night. The good odds supported my hopes, but the way I was told these odds carried the message that my fears were not legitimate.

The idea of good odds is one of the ways medicine defines chemotherapy as simply an "incident." The medical staff's descriptions of chemotherapy always minimized the suffering. One day when my side effects were particularly bad I was lying in a bed in day care, doing what patients do best, which is wait. On the other side of the curtain a physician was giving another patient the same introduction to chemotherapy speech I remembered from a couple of months earlier. Chemotherapy was presented as merely a transitory inconvenience: no need to take much time off from work, there will be hair loss but nothing else serious, just a couple of months, and so on. I had a wicked desire to pull back the curtain and say, "Yes, and you'll look like this." That patient did not need to know everything in advance; still, he had a right to be told enough to allow him to do some realistic planning. More important, he had a right to have affirmed that what he was going through was no small thing. Instead he was being cued not to take his experience seriously, and that is what I wish I could have changed.

Many people have far longer chemotherapies than I had, with far worse chances of recovery. It may become easy for those who work in cancer centers to think of chemotherapy for testicular cancer as merely a transitory inconvenience. Unfortunately, this attitude denies ill persons the validity and importance of what we experience. The three months of chemotherapy seemed like a lifetime to me, in part because of my fear that it might be the end of my life, but also because of the suffering I acknowledged and the adventure I found.

The chemotherapy used for testicular cancer was first described to me as one of the "most aggressive" treatments given. I had this image of five brawny guys throwing me on a bed and starting an IV. The aggressiveness, of course, refers to the toxicity of the drugs and the severity of their side effects. Although hair loss is the side effect most often associated with chemotherapy, far more discomforting were the nausea, gum soreness, constipation, and, perhaps most intense although brief, the burning pain while urinating. A more important side effect is the destruction of the white cells that are the basis of the immune system. Although this causes no discomfort, it increases the person's vulnerability to sickness; I lived in fear that sickness would disrupt the schedule of chemotherapy.

Beyond these specific side effects, chemotherapy leaves the body feeling wrecked. This is not surprising, since it is nothing more than toxic drugs killing the body's cells. How it made me feel can be compared with the effect my two operations had on me. Even though I had no conscious memory of pain while under anesthetic, my body retained a sense of what had been done to it. Something had happened to me, and even if I couldn't quite remember it, I knew it had been awful. Chemotherapy involved no real pain, but my body again knew something awful was being done to it.

If anyone reading this book is about to have chemotherapy, she should realize that these side effects vary depending on the individual and the treatment. Improvements are being made in the drugs to counter the side effects, and the treatments themselves change. The details of my treatment are part of my own story, *not* a guide to what others can expect.

Each chemotherapy treatment was administered over three days, during which I was an inpatient in the cancer center. I was given different drugs intravenously according to a specific time schedule. The sequencing had to be exact, because each drug kills cancer cells at different stages of their development. The number of treatments varies. Not long before my illness patients were usually given six treatments, but I had three. Some recent research suggests that one treatment may be fully effective. The drugs seem to do as much the first time as they are ever going to. As attractive as the idea of having only one treatment is, I was not sure, even during chemotherapy, that I wanted to be the first to get less than the usual course. I had lived with the fear of cancer for so long that finally being treated gave me a sense of security.

Between treatments I went home, returning to the cancer center each week for blood tests and medication to relieve side effects. I felt the worst physical effects from the second day after I got home until about a week later. Within a week I could read without nausea, though still without much concentration. My appetite returned with a vengeance, and my mouth soreness lessened enough to allow me to eat. In the remaining ten days or so before my next treatment I lived as normal a life as I could with constant medical appointments and no immune system. About the time I began to feel fairly good, my white blood cell count was high enough for another round of chemotherapy. We began again.

Two weeks after each treatment I also had a CAT (computerized axial tomography) scan to determine if the tumors along my back had decreased in size. The progress of this decrease determined when chemotherapy would stop, so I did not know if my third treatment was my last until the scan two weeks afterward. After a certain point the tumors did not shrink any further, and my cancer center assumed that what was left was scar tissue. I was scanned for a year after treatment to confirm that no tumors were growing.

The CAT scans were not pleasant. In movies the patient is wafted through a high-tech donut with lights flashing all round. In reality it is less entertaining. The night before a scan I had to take massive laxatives to empty my intestines. At most I got two hours of sleep. During the scan I had a barium enema, and sometimes an intravenous needle in my arm put another contrast fluid into the circulatory system. The scans are obviously less "invasive" than surgery, but during the procedure I felt invaded enough. With the enema and the IV going, you lie absolutely still for about thirty minutes, holding your arms above your head while passing through an X-ray that takes a sequence of cross-sectional pictures. These provide an exact image of the internal organs and, in my case, tumors.

Chemotherapy has a terrible reputation, but my own aggressive treatment had no special horrors. It was a series of mundane discomforts, one after another, with no rest. The drugs and the hospital rooms induced a sense of claustrophobia, heightened by the two IV lines that ran into me, one for the chemotherapy drugs themselves and the other for anti-nausea drugs. The latter were effective, but they left me too disoriented for real conversation. I slept irregularly. When I was awake, time passed in minutes. The drugs dissociated me from my body's usual feedback; drugged, I lived in an "it." Mostly it felt restless but also as though moving would make me seriously nauseated.

These IVs did not involve needles because I had undergone a second operation to install a "central line" or permanent catheter. One end of a tube was placed directly in my heart, and the other end passed under the skin up by the collarbone and down across the chest, exiting just below the ribs, with about a foot of tubing coming out. When I was not having an IV, the tubing was taped to my chest. Catheters for single IVs sit just below the skin, but I was going to be given such large doses of drugs that a two-IV model was necessary. The purpose of the central line was to prevent veins from collapsing because of the toxicity of the chemotherapy drugs, and also to provide for better dispersion of the drugs through the body.

Thus my three months of chemotherapy were spent with a foot of tubing hanging out of my chest. The line became part of my body, but the body was no longer entirely mine. The line was a symbol of cancer that I wore on my body; even when I felt pretty good, there it was, reminding me of all the aspects of cancer. I was vulnerable because it carried the risk of infection, and I was dependent on it during treatment. Through it chemotherapy drugs went in and blood samples came out.

The line was another flag planted by the medical system on my body. I resented it as much as I needed it. My tolerance for pain had been chipped away, first by the tumors that woke me at night and later by such mundane hospital annoyances as being wakened each morning for blood tests. Blood tests are no big thing, but when you are woken every day by someone sticking a needle into your arm several times, this too drains your resistance to discomfort.

I needed the line not only for relief from pain, but also as a way of displacing my larger fears about cancer. I was able to refocus these fears — whether chemotherapy was working, how long it would go on — onto the daily problems of managing the line. If cancer itself was too much to worry about, I could worry instead about the line. Because the exit site is an open wound, it could become infected. The line might malfunction and fail to draw blood properly, although I had no such problems with it. But I never had full use of my right arm; too much movement would cause the line to pull.

The line also refocused the relationship Cathie and I had fallen into. By the time it was installed, the hospital had pretty well taken me over. Although Cathie was usually with me during physician's visits, the doctors and nurses never acknowledged her presence. Medical staff talked to me even if they found it difficult to make eye contact with me; they treated Cathie like a nonperson. She and I observed this and even joked about it, but it wore on us. Hospitals separate physical treatment from emotional care; caregivers are treated like an optional luxury, pleasant for the patient to have around but not necessary to treatment. Cathie and I were having a hard time resisting being split into patient and visitor.

Physical care requires emotional support, and emotional support needs physical involvement, which the line provided. The exit site had to be disinfected and bandaged daily, and during the intervals between chemotherapy treatments, the line had to be flushed with saline solution. Cathie took over the disinfecting, flushing, and bandaging, and these tasks became a daily ritual between us. We laughed that it was "our special time" together, but those moments of quiet in a hectic life were a gift. My illness had not decreased the normal demands of our lives, particularly of her life, and had added many demands of its own. Soon the procedure with the line became routine, and we were able to talk while Cathie went through the motions. Illness can crowd out talk. The time spent maintaining the line each day, even if it was yet another of cancer's demands, was one way of finding new terms for our relationship. When I went back to being an inpatient, Cathie and I joked about how much better her antiseptic procedures were than those of the nurses who dressed the line. At least between ourselves, she was no longer a visitor.

*

Chemotherapy accentuates the basic challenge presented by illness: how to continue to live when your life has been altered so radically. It turned life into a bizarre roller coaster of destruction and recovery, repeated three times. A new side effect would require a different medication, or some other worry would need attention. But behind these mundane problems lurked the only real issue: would it be effective? Would I be one of the lucky 80 percent who come out alive? And behind the danger that I might die was the danger that even while I was alive I might be worn away by what was happening.

The danger of chemotherapy is that you may lose the sense of value in your life; you may fade into the claustrophobia and passivity of treatment and become so obsessed with details of bodily care that your mind shares the numbness of your body. The opportunity is to discover new sources of value in familiar things too often ignored. Although my side effects were worse when I was at home, I could live with them because of what it meant to be at home. Getting out of the hospital always seemed like a rebirth. Hospitals deprive the senses; outside I was aware of real air and colors and textures, variations of light and the noise of a normal world going about its business. At home there were cards and calls from friends and family. I heard from people I had not seen in years and was surprised they even knew I had cancer. These messages in particular gave me what I think ill persons need most, a sense that many others, more than you can think of, care deeply that you live. Most of all, home was where Cathie and I could be together in a place that was ours.

But at home as in the hospital, the ill person is eventually alone with illness. Then what was I to think about all that was happening to me? What was I to make of myself, vulnerable, dependent, my body often unable to eat or excrete? I never thought up any answers to these questions, but some answers found me. Unsought and unexpected, a sense of adventure came to me from two very different places.

In our living room we have a lithograph that was given to me years ago, a poster by Marc Chagall for a show in Paris in the 1960s. The theme of the show was Chagall's biblical art, and in the lithograph Jacob is being blessed by the angel. On days when I was able to do little more than sit, I watched the afternoon light pass through the room and gazed at the Chagall. Here is the biblical text:

> And Jacob was left alone; and there wrestled a man with him until the breaking of the day.
>
> And when he saw that he prevailed not against him, he touched the hollow of his thigh; and the hollow of Jacob's thigh was out of joint, as he wrestled with him.
>
> And he said, Let me go, for the day breaketh. And he said, I will not let thee go, except thou bless me.
>
> And he said unto him, What is thy name? And he said, Jacob.
>
> And he said, thy name shall be called no more Jacob, but Israel: for as a prince hast thou power with God and with men, and hast prevailed.
>
> And Jacob asked him, and said, Tell me, I pray thee, thy name. And he said, Wherefore is it that thou dost ask after my name? And he blessed him there.
>
> And Jacob called the name of the place Peniel: for I have seen God face to face, and my life is preserved.

And as he passed over Peniel the sun rose upon him, and he halted upon his thigh. (Genesis 32:24–30)

Stories we tell ourselves about what is happening to us are dangerous because they are powerful. Stories come to us from many sources; some we seek, many happen without our notice, others impose themselves on our lives. We have to choose carefully which stories to live with, which to use to answer the question of what is happening to us. Jacob's wrestling became a story I lived with as part of my personal mythology of illness. This is what it is to be ill: to wrestle through the long night, injured, and if you prevail until the sun rises, to receive a blessing. Through Jacob's story, illness became an adventure.

Other stories found their way into this personal mythology of illness as adventure. It was the autumn when Paul Simon's album "Graceland" was popular. Pop music at its best has an openness that allows the listener to believe it was written just for him. A story that is anyone's can become yours. As I sat pumped full of chemicals, my immune system as close to gone as the doctors dared drive it, Simon's "The Boy in the Bubble" became mine.

> These are the days of miracles and wonder
> This is the long distance call
> The way the camera follows us in slo-mo
> The way we look to us all
> The way we look to a distant constellation
> That's dying in a corner of the sky
> These are the days of miracles and wonder
> And don't cry baby don't cry
> Don't cry

It seemed easy to cry during those days. But between Jacob's angel and Simon's miracles and wonder, I found a sense of adventure in illness. My body was a toxic waste dump, but it was also living a miracle. Twenty years before, maybe even ten, I would have been dying instead of getting chemotherapy. Now the ultimate slo-mo of the CAT scan cameras showed the tumors shrinking. My existence was a wonder, living it an adventure. I could believe in prevailing until the sun rose. The blessing was that I was seeing life, face to face.

The Struggle Is Not a Fight

PEOPLE with other diseases are just plain sick; those with cancer "fight" it. During my heart trouble no one suggested I fight my heart, but one of the first things I was told about cancer was, "You have to fight." Read any set of obituaries. People die of cancer after a "valiant battle" or a "long bout." Government research programs are "wars" on cancer. Newspaper stories that refer to poverty, crime, and drug abuse as "cancers" reflect society's attitude toward cancer as the dreaded other. Against this other, combat is the only appropriate response. But I do not believe illness should be lived as a fight.

The fight metaphor does capture something of what living with illness is like. Cathie and I talked about cancer as a life during wartime. We did not mean we were waging a war against the enemy, cancer. Rather we were searching for words to describe lives that had been overrun. We thought of ourselves as civilians whose home had become a battlefield. Demands and crises followed one after the other so fast that we felt buffeted. As soon as we worked through the emotions of one crisis we were "hit" by another, ranging from a new side effect of chemotherapy to a feared infection of my line. Medical appointments conflicted with the demands of our jobs. As someone put it, illness is one damn thing after another. Pervading all of it, always, is the fear of dying. So life during wartime seemed an appropriate description.

But our talk never suggested that we were fighting cancer. We never thought of "the cancer" as a thing to be fought. That would have personified it, and it is this personification I object to. Cancer is not some entity separate from yourself. As I lay in my hospital room awaiting surgery, I had to find some way to understand these tumors inside me. Were they something alien, smuggled in from outside and not really part of me? Or were they as much a part of me as my brain and muscles?

Most people opt for the tumor-as-alien. At the extreme, Ronald Reagan's well-known statement about his cancer, "I don't have cancer. I had something inside of me that had cancer in it, and it was removed," sums up this unwillingness to understand cancer as part of oneself. I only hope this served Reagan well. For myself, I had cancer.

The tumors may have been a painful part of me, they may have threatened my life, but they were still me. They were part of a body that would not function much longer unless it changed, but that body was still who I was. I could never split my body into two warring camps: the bad guy tumors opposed to the naturally healthy me. There was only one me, one body, tumors and all. Accepting that I was still one body brought me a great sense of relief.

The tumors had to go if the body was to survive, but this was the body's problem. My consciousness could not make the tumors go away any more than it had brought them. Consciously I could only wonder at the body and accept its wisdom. I could desire to live, but life itself was more than I could take responsibility for. As soon as I gave up fighting myself and let my body change according to its wisdom — with some additional direction from surgery and chemotherapy — I felt far more peaceful. There was no fight, only the possibility of change. Making this possibility real involved suffering and struggle, but not fighting. Thinking of tumors as enemies and the body as a battlefield is not a gentle attitude toward oneself, and ill persons have only enough energy for gentleness. Aggression is misplaced energy. You may feel anger because of the way you are treated, but that is different from fighting yourself.

Though I did not personify my tumors, it seemed useful to visualize them. This process had nothing to do with fighting cancer. I simply allowed images of the tumors to appear, with as little conscious direction as possible, and visualized them disappearing. Actually I visualized my white blood cells more often than my tumors. In normal times white cells "kill" the cancer cells the body constantly produces. I imagined the white cells, but an image of them attacking the tumors never came to me. They were simply there, on guard, standing silhouetted on mountain cliffs. My imagination gave the white cells the form of ancient Greek soldiers, perhaps because my white cell count reminded me of the number of Greeks at the battle of Marathon, a word that has particular connotations for me as a runner.

I had learned many times that running a marathon is a struggle but it cannot be a fight. You cannot fight for twenty-six miles; it's too far. At least for a middle-aged recreational runner the trick in marathon running is to coddle the body. If you treat yourself as gently as possible, your body's energy will unfold over the distance. In the far reaches you may realize sources of energy you never knew the body had. The body knows how to run; you have to learn to let it.

During cancer I tried to let my body do what it wanted with the tumors. The white cells, my Greek guards, were there, watching. The tumors had no identity, no faces, hardly even shapes. Flaccid and without purpose, they were vulnerable. They had no basis for survival. It wasn't necessary to "attack" them; they simply disappeared. The tumors were superfluous. My life was ready to move on and had no time for them.

I confess that I did ask myself how the tumors had gotten there to begin with. I do not recommend such thinking. It seems better to believe that cancer just happens. But at the time I could not resist asking "why me?" And this question led me to a sense of past inadequacy. A woman I know who has ovarian cancer believes that it was caused by an antinausea drug she took when she was pregnant. Unlike most of us, she can ask herself "why me?" and find answers that are not fantasies of self-blame. But for those who do not have such a direct physiological cause, the answer to "why me?" is bound to involve guilt. As the prayer I learned as a child in church said, "We have left undone those things which we ought to have done, And we have done those things which we ought not to have done, And" — here's the punchline — "there is no health in us." What terrible words to put in the mind of a child! It becomes all too easy for an ill person to work backward: If there is no health in me, then I must have done something wrong or at least left something undone.

This kind of confessional thinking led me to all sorts of regrets. It is proper to meditate on how you have lived so that you can become the person you want to be. But it is a sad mistake to believe that cancer is caused by something you have or have not done. To believe my own inadequacies were so spectacular that they gave me cancer is just vanity.

As a bodily process, cancer "just happened" to me. The explanations I like best are fairly medical. During my embryonic development, some of the cellular processes went wrong. Perhaps they went wrong in a way that would produce testicular cancer no matter what else happened to me. Perhaps this cellular time bomb was waiting for some stress or some virus or some combination of toxins we don't understand yet. Maybe someday the process will be controlled, just as someday we may understand the subtle and indirect ways that the mind can influence both the disease and the cure of the body. But at our present level of knowledge, cancer of the type I had just happens.

But if I did not do anything that caused cancer, neither am I just a pawn in some random draw of bodies destined to become diseased. As soon as cancer happened to me, not just to anyone, it ceased to be random. I am a bodily process, but I am also a consciousness, with a will and a history and a capacity to focus my thoughts and energies. The bodily process and the consciousness do not oppose each other; what illness teaches is their unity. The mind gives meaning to what happens in the body, but the mind also thinks through the body it is a part of. The mind does not simply contemplate itself in a body with cancer. As cancer reshapes that body, the mind changes in response to the disease's effects. Pain taught me the body's power to shape thinking. But my thinking was shaping the pain even as it was being shaped by that pain — the circle is unbroken.

Illness is a physical process and an experience, each shaping the other. The physical process just happens to me; the experience is my responsibility. What my body does in the last five miles of a marathon just happens, but what just happens has been shaped by a lifetime of choosing to use that body in particular ways. In my body's will I recognize my will, and it goes beyond consciousness, while still including that consciousness.

We cannot fight cancer or tumors. We can only trust the body's will and get as much medical help as we can. We form the body's will through years of conscious acts, but in the end what finally happens just happens. I still believe there is great health in us, but we also die some day. I am not powerful enough to feel either guilty for getting sick or proud of getting well. I can only take what happens to me and continue to look for possibilities of how to live.

Writing about the value of not fighting takes me back to Jacob wrestling with the angel. The story is about a man fighting for his soul, but we have to look carefully at how this fight proceeds. For me, the other whom Jacob wrestles is himself. Jacob's personal history is checkered, to say the least. He begins by stealing his father's blessing from his older brother, Esau, who rightly should have had it. Jacob is then tricked by his father-in-law into marrying the wrong sister. After various deceptions and escapes, Jacob is finally alone. At that moment in his life, he could easily believe there were two of him: his good self and his "dark twin," who stole Esau's blessing and generated the other troubles that followed. This dark twin is the character whom various mythologies call the trickster. Jacob has to decide which side of him will prevail, the servant of God or his dark twin, the trickster.

The wrestling is a struggle but not a fight. Jacob wins not by defeating his darker side, but by realizing that the other he is contesting shares the face of God. Jacob does not overcome his opponent; instead he finds divinity in him. The outcome of the wrestling match is twofold. Jacob leaves with a wound: "The sun rose upon him, and he halted upon his thigh." He also gains a blessing: The servant of God wins for himself the prize the trickster first stole, but perhaps the blessing is that now the two have become one. Wounded, Jacob becomes whole. Whole, he is renamed.

Illness is not a fight against an other, but it is a long struggle. Some prevail by continuing to live; some prevail in dying. Those who are ill and those who witness illness can only have faith in the wholeness of either outcome. Faith must displace will, just as struggling with cancer must displace fighting against it.

Being ill is a perpetual balancing of faith and will. I find this quality of faith in the stories of Jacob and other Old Testament characters attempting to serve what they call God's will. It is a will outside of themselves that, in my language, just happens to them. When Moses is asked to lead the Hebrews from Egypt, or when Abraham is told to sacrifice Isaac, or when Noah builds an ark, they must accept what just seems to happen. This quality of acceptance is what I call faith.

But faith is hardly resignation. Acceptance requires each to achieve something. Jacob most actively wrestles with a paradox: a will that is his but is other than his own. He discovers that even his trickster self has the face of God, and in this paradoxical discovery he becomes whole.

Diseases are not messages from some god, nor is illness a test of faith. These ideas are among the dangers of a mythology that also has opportunities. The opportunity is to recognize that although illness just happens, we can organize its experience to make our lives meaningful. We can have both a faith that allows us to accept whatever just happens and at the same time a will to bring about the change we desire. Thus I find no contradiction between leaving illness to the body's will and seeking medical help. We are most faithful when active, just as we struggle best when we do not fight.

Stigma

WHENEVER I told someone I had cancer I felt myself tighten as I said it. Saying the word "cancer," my body began to defend itself. This did not happen when I told people I was having heart problems. A heart attack was simply bad news. But I never stopped thinking that cancer said something about my worth as a person. This difference between heart attack and cancer is stigma. A stigma is, literally, a sign on the surface of the body marking it as dangerous, guilty, and unclean. Stigmas began as judicial punishments in the form of notched ears, brandings, and other visible mutilations of the body. These marks allowed those who came into contact with the stigmatized person to see whom they were dealing with. The stigmatized were expected to go to the margins of society and hide their spoiled bodies. The causes of stigmatization have changed, but the hiding has not.

My heart attack damaged my body but did not stigmatize it. I became short of breath while doing tasks that were normal for a man my age. This was inconvenient and embarrassing but not stigmatizing. The damaged body only fails to perform properly; the stigmatized body contaminates its surroundings. During my heart problems I could no longer participate in certain activities; during cancer I felt I had no right to be among others. As much as I disliked being in the hospital, at least there I felt I belonged. I knew this was foolish. I didn't belong in the hospital; I was hiding there. Ill persons hide in many ways. Some begin to call cancer "c.a.," "the big C," or other euphemisms. I called it cancer, but as I said it I felt that tightness.

Heart attacks are invisible on the body's surface. To myself and to others, I looked no different. One wears cancer. My own visible stigmas were hair loss and my intravenous line. The line created a bulge over my chest, but I could conceal it. Getting dressed each day became an exercise in concealment. I wore shirts that were heavy and loose fitting and equally loose sweaters. A tie under the sweater added some bulk, and a sport coat further obscured the contours of my body. The question, of course, is why I wanted to hide the line from others. The sad answer is that I experienced the visible signs of cancer as defects not just in my appearance, but in myself.

The visible sign most closely associated with cancer is hair loss. Alopecia, or baldness, is caused not by cancer itself but by its treatment. Chemotherapy is not very discriminating. Cancer cells divide rapidly, but so do the cells of hair follicles, the intestinal lining, and gums. The drugs destroy cells in all these areas, creating their particular side effects. Thus there is truth to the folk wisdom that baldness indicates chemotherapy is working. Even knowing this, my enthusiasm for losing my hair was qualified.

My hair fell out several days after my first chemotherapy

treatment. First it lost its texture and became thin, then the hair on the sides of my head rubbed off while I was washing it. I was left with a patchy-looking mohawk. It was almost Halloween, but I resisted the temptation to turn my appearance into a punk costume.

Some people try to preserve what hair they have for as long as they can. I thought I looked stranger with some hair than I would with none. Also we got tired of cleaning out the tub and drain every time I took a shower; hot water speeds up the hair loss. So Cathie helped me shave off the rest of my hair, which was truly a labor of love. That shaving marked my full passage into another stage of illness, and it was a sad thing. The loss of hair has to be mourned; it is another break with the younger self you no longer are.

To be completely bald at my age was a bit unusual, but it was not in itself stigmatizing. I had never thought of hair loss as one of life's great problems. But losing my hair all at once was traumatic, even if my age and gender reduced the trauma. For women and some younger males the loss would be different, but not entirely different. The actual hair loss bothered me less than what this loss meant. Cancer made baldness into a stigma; I imagined others seeing me as a cancer "victim." Baldness was a reduction to the passivity of a victim, a patient, or a sufferer. Even a woman who normally wore a wig would feel this stigma, given her present reason for that wig.

The first week without hair was physically unpleasant and emotionally difficult. My newly bald head was extremely sensitive to touch and cold. Even a pillowcase felt rough to skin that had never been exposed to direct touch. I had to sleep on a soft towel. The normal drafts in our house felt like a wind tunnel on my head. This physical unpleasantness lasted only a few days, but the stigma remained.

I took to wearing a hat. In part this was for warmth; November turned cold that year, and I quickly realized how much insulation even short hair provides. But I also used the hat to give others a chance to adjust their reactions as they saw that I had no hair around the sides and then realized I had none at all. I grew fond of my hat, but I also needed its protection. I had a dark fantasy, which many stigmatized persons have in one form or another. My fear was that someday, somewhere, someone would see my bald head and scream, "Oh my god, he has cancer!" Looking back on that time, I was the one who was screaming.

Gradually I began leaving the hat off, at first around the office and then at concerts and such. But I did not lose my sense of stigma until after chemotherapy ended. As I became confident that I was in remission, my self-consciousness disappeared. The only time I actually heard anyone talking about my baldness was about six weeks after the end of chemotherapy, when my head was developing a five o'clock shadow. I was standing in a line and heard a woman telling a child that maybe I was in the army, where they cut their hair very short. I smiled to myself. By then baldness was nothing more than the absence of hair. The cause of the stigma had disappeared when I went into remission and was no longer a cancer patient; the visible sign had lost its meaning. I was just a bald, middle-aged college professor who could still pass as an army recruit.

During active treatment I never found a way of dealing with my sense of stigma. Like the experience of pain, stigma ended before I resolved it. I do not think I could ever have resolved it alone. If the person with cancer can believe that other people's phobias about cancer are their problem, fine, but this thought brings little comfort to those who feel stigmatized. Telling people to hang tough only works for those who already are.

The idea that cancer represents a defect in the ill person's identity does not go away easily. Society imposes this idea on us every day in subtle ways. The newspapers recently carried a story about an advertising model who once portrayed the macho image of the Winston man in that tobacco company's advertisements. He quit smoking and now works for health promotion groups that are trying to eliminate cigarettes. One reason for the change was that his brother got lung cancer. In the article the man's visit to his brother in the hospital was reduced to a description of seeing all these "guys without hair." The loss, suffering, and fear that go with cancer were reduced to the most visible symbol, the bald head. Of course, pain and death are too much for our imaginations; hair loss is immediately understood. It becomes the part of cancer we can grasp when the whole overwhelms us.

The newspaper story subtly reconfirms the stigma of baldness. It links a voluntary behavior, smoking, to cancer, whose dominant sign is baldness. Wrong action produces the disease, and the disease is reduced to its visual sign. I admire what the former model is doing, and I support the antismoking message of the story. But we are left with an unfortunate moral allegory: the man saved from the damnation of smoking by seeing his brother's fall into cancer. It's a health promotion version of Dickens's "A Christmas Carol," with the brother as Marley's ghost, telling the Winston man to reform or end up like him. Since the days of notched ears, the power of stigma has fed on seeing the body's condition as an expression of morality, and this linkage is virtually irresistible to our thinking. The story is one example of how society defines stigmas. Because AIDS is now the most stigmatized disease, persons with AIDS understand how society imposes stigmas on individuals. I believe all ill persons, particularly those with cancer, have much to learn from persons with AIDS. Because many of them had been politically active in the gay rights movement, they knew that society's response to disease is a political issue. They first insisted on being called "persons with AIDS" instead of patients, victims, or sufferers. The shift in language marks a change to thinking of oneself as active, not passive; thus I write about persons with cancer, except when they are specifically patients. At times a person with cancer may be a patient or a victim (of a carcinogenic drug, for example), or a sufferer. But what matters most, no matter what you call yourself or are called, is that you remain foremost a person, actively living your life.

Resisting stigmatization requires more than individual will. Ill persons who cannot brush off stigmatization as someone else's problem need to organize themselves. The prospect of hanging tough against stigma may not be comforting to one who must do it alone, but as a group people can hang tough. The problem is that organizations of ill persons are often not supported by institutional medicine. In some cancer centers self-help organizations are restricted or prohibited from visiting patients to make them aware of what support is available. Because organizations of ill persons often define treatment issues as political, they make demands that hospitals do not want to hear. Institutions find it easier to manage patients who think of themselves as isolated and are thus passive. Society is obsessed with "health," but it prefers to keep ill persons on its margins, making them as invisible as possible. When people are stigmatized, they hide themselves.

Cancer can do terrible things to the body, but so can other diseases. Cultural historians tell us that for at least a century cancer has been North Americans' most feared disease. This fear is explained only partially by either actual rates of cancer incidence and mortality or by the physical suffering it causes. Society, not the disease itself, makes cancer as dreaded as it is. A culture in which people are unwilling to speak the name of the disease obviously has a special fear. We do not call heart attack "h.a." Cancer alone is mythologized as some savage god, whose very name will invoke its presence. If the name of cancer is unspeakable, what evil does the person with cancer believe can be brought by his presence? Newspaper stories and political speeches use cancer as the metaphor for all the worst that can happen. The ill person then becomes the bearer of these horrors. Just as I tried to hide my intravenous line under my coat, persons with cancer want to hide their disease. Never have I tried so hard to be invisible.

To lose the sense of stigma, persons with cancer must come in from the margins and be visible. Organizations of ill persons are one form of visibility; I hope this book will be another. Stigmatization will be overcome only when we learn to witness the experience of cancer, not hide it. Every attempt to hide cancer, every euphemism, every concealment, reconfirms that the stigma is real and deserved. When I heard that woman explaining my shaved hair to a child, it was a personal victory for me to be able to smile. It would have been a social victory if I had walked over and said, "No, actually I'm recovering from cancer, but it's all right; cancer's only another disease, and diseases are only human." That would have broken the cycle of stigma.

Denial and Affirmation

PEOPLE DID NOT ACT that differently toward me while I had cancer, they only exaggerated how they had always acted. The compassionate ones became more loving, the generous more giving, the ill at ease more defensive. The bullies were peskier than usual, and the ones who were always too busy remained busy. Some people whom I expected to be supportive denied that I was ill at all; medical staff denied that I was anything but the disease. Others affirmed that although I was ill and illness counted, we still had a relationship. These denials and affirmations were not always easy to recognize as they happened. Denials can be subtle; after being with someone I would feel bad and not be sure why.

But illness also exaggerated the ways I acted toward others. I needed other people desperately but, feeling stigmatized, I was cautious of them. One day I would express closeness, the next day distance. My behavior caused others to exaggerate their responses to me, and in my perception of them I exaggerated their actions still further. Even the strongest relationships came under stress. This is how the ill person experiences others during illness: subtle denials, strained affirmations.

The most subtle denials may be those of cancer itself. One day Cathie and I were appreciating a nurse's interest in us until she said to Cathie, "Oh, your mother died of c.a. too." And there it was again: another refusal to say the dreaded c-word. She undoubtedly thought she was protecting us; nurses are very keen on "not upsetting the patient." But if that is the explanation, why do nurses use these euphemisms among themselves when no patients are around to become upset? Cathie and I have both worked on the "professional" side of hospitals enough to know that the patient's presence does not determine how nurses speak, or don't speak, of cancer.

More important than the nurse's motive was that I experienced her "c.a." as a denial. I was waiting to be examined because I feared I was having a recurrence of cancer. Although I did not welcome it, I was working hard to think that if cancer was happening again, I would live with it. Then the nurse's refusal to say the word "cancer" told me that what might be happening to my body was too awful to be called by its proper name. I was suddenly ashamed of what might be wrong with me. In the silencing of the word "cancer," I as a person with cancer was also silenced. It was the same silencing I had experienced when Cathie told me about the nurse who referred to me as the "seminoma in 53." She denied that I existed as anything more than the disease. Now even the disease was unspeakable. In that nurse's "c.a." I disappeared.

Suffering also is denied. Those who provide treatment give patients cues as to the emotions that are appropriate to express. Because patients are dependent on medical staff, they tend to accept these cues. Nurses and physicians cue patients to deny their own experience when they compare one patient's suffering to that of someone who is "much worse off." Comparisons deny the uniqueness of each individual's experience. As losses, disfigurements, pains are compared, a standard emerges against which the suffering of each individual is measured. Compared to the suffering of the "worst case," my experiences are devalued. This logic makes it possible to find the one person, first in the hospital, eventually in the world, who is *the* worst off. Only that "designated complainer" would have any right to express discomfort, unhappiness, fear, or any other "negative" emotion.

Ill persons deserve better. My suffering cannot be compared to yours or to anyone else's; it can only be witnessed for what it is. When I talk to other persons with cancer, we do not compare frequency of nausea, duration of hair loss, or length of scars. Persons with cancer respect each other's experiences. They recognize that having cancer is no small thing.

Medical staff who make comparisons are trapped by a belief that unless they can do something to reduce the bodily suffering, they have failed as professionals. Continuing suffering threatens them, so they deny it exists. What they cannot treat, the patient is not allowed to experience. Physicians and nurses often forget that when treatment runs out, there can still be care. Simply recognizing suffering for what it is, regardless of whether it can be treated, is care.

Professionals can and do care, but when they do they are acting a bit unprofessional. When my diagnosis was uncertain, one medical resident spent some time just letting me talk. Our talk wasn't related to treatment; he listened to my fears and shared his own. Later his supervisor advised him that once symptoms and history have been elicited, further talk with patients is considered unproductive. Sadly, the standard of what is "professional" often denies the opportunity for care.

The only way I could get my surgeon, a seasoned professional, to talk to me about the details of and alternatives to the operation he was planning (which was never carried out and would have been unnecessary) was to refuse to sign the consent form. In effect I denied his denial. We then had a long conversation. His knowledge and experience helped me, but this help came only after I had hit him with the only two-by-four a patient has. Or perhaps, in the inverted world of hospitals, my not signing permitted him to have the kind of contact he would like to have with patients but cannot justify.

The denials an ill person faces do not stop with treatment. The institutions for which most of us work deny that people have bodies and that life requires attention to these bodies. Institutions consider bodies only as resources for production, not as lives being lived. Thus the sympathy an ill person receives has institutional limits. While I was in active treatment, the university where I work was most solicitous. Arrangements were made for others to teach my classes when I was too ill, and my department sent flowers to the hospital. People I worked with expressed concern for me.

But as soon as treatment ended, the other institutional face appeared. Some of the same people now asked for the work I was supposed to have been doing. It didn't count that I had been ill; in the annual assessment written about each faculty member, the time of my illness was described as showing a "lack of scholarly productivity." I had to remind the administrator who wrote the report to specify that this lack was due to illness. But illness does not matter for institutions, any more than pregnancy matters or caring for someone else who is ill matters. Careers are not supposed to show gaps. When life is understood as a career, the résumé becomes an extension of the body. Gaps in the résumé are institutional stigmas. Since most of us have to work, it is hard for ill persons to resist accepting "productivity" as the measure of our worth.

In all these experiences people denied what I was going through or had been through, and the one medical resident who did not deny was told he should have. The sad logic of such denials is that the ill person ends up feeling guilty for the disease, the suffering, or the low productivity.

The ultimate denial is by friends and loved ones who simply disappear from the ill person's life. In disappearing, they deny that anything special is happening or, alternatively, that the ill person exists at all. Either form of denial can be truly devastating. If I asked these people why they disappeared from Cathie's life and mine during cancer, they would probably say they were busy, they did not want to bother us, and they "knew" we would call if we needed anything. But what we needed was to hear they cared. Such people can't see what their behavior looks like to the ill person and those who are caring for him or her. At Christmas, just after a chemotherapy treatment, I was at a small family gathering but was still too weak to get up and circulate among the guests. Someone I had felt close to arrived, a man I had not heard from during my illness. He did not come to the end of the room where I was sitting and did his best not to look in my direction. Perhaps I was too vulnerable to go to him or just too tired, or perhaps I felt, as I do now, that it was his responsibility to come to me.

A relative tried to excuse the behavior of some of the people who disappeared from Cathie's and my life during cancer by saying that they "cared silently at a distance." We know cancer is hard for people to confront, but from the perspective of the ill person and caregivers, "caring silently" might as well not be happening. Their distance looks like another denial of the illness. Just as I had expected that physicians would behave differently if I became critically ill, I also expected something more from family and friends. My expectations weren't always met; although the generous became more giving, the busy were still too busy.

Those who best affirmed my experience were often people who had been through critical illness themselves or with someone close. We did not necessarily talk a great deal about specific experiences, but these friends seemed able to look at me clearly and to accept what they saw. They rarely tried to cheer me up, but being with them usually did cheer me. Human suffering becomes bearable when we share it. When we know that someone recognizes our pain, we can let go of it. The power of recognition to reduce suffering cannot be explained, but it seems fundamental to our humanity.

People can recognize the experience of the ill in many ways. We needed the friends who called, brought food, sent cards, and took Cathie to lunch. They affirmed that we were still there and had needs. I write "we" because in many of these affirmations, as in many of the denials, an action toward me or toward Cathie affected the other one equally.

Cathie remains the caregiver whose affirmations mean the most to me. When it was becoming certain that I had cancer, she put her arms around me and told me she needed my survival, that her life required mine. I took the strength I needed from her and survived, but at a cost to her. Society organizes illness so that every demand is put on those who care for the ill. Someone is expected to get the patient to treatment, fill the prescriptions, notify friends and family of news, clean and supply the house, coordinate with the ill person's employer, change bandages and do other medical tasks at home, be a pleasant and loving visitor in the hospital, get the oil changed in the car, and ask the physician the questions the patient is too drugged to remember. Once during chemotherapy Cathie noticed that the nurse had reversed the suction on the intravenous pump, so that it was drawing blood rather than pumping in drugs. The responsibilities of the caregiver have no bounds.

But neither hospitals in particular nor society in general recognize or support the caregiver. Hospital spaces and schedules are designed to treat diseases; they do not accommodate people trying to sustain relationships while illness is tearing apart their lives. When medical staff need assistance, they expect the caregiver to be on call; otherwise he or she is a visitor. Medicine assumes that the person who has the disease is the only one who is ill. This assumption is shared by other institutions and even by family and friends, who should realize that illness is an experience that a couple has together — each differently, but one no less than the other.

I remember the night early in my illness when I looked in the mirror and thought of all I was going to lose before it was over. But I, we, did not realize that Cathie might lose even more. Few people who have not had a critical illness seem to recognize the danger and the losses to the caregiver. The notion of disease gave me some excuse for my absences from work; Cathie had as many added demands but none of the excuses. Some colleagues who praised her efforts caring for me and for her mother would then ask her for the work she was supposed to be doing during this time, the "real" work as opposed to the work of caring for others. The ill person has no choice but to give up status as a result of time "lost." The caregiver willingly accepts the personal costs of giving time and energy to the ill person. That most caregivers are women makes society's nonrecognition of caring a central cause of women's disadvantage in jobs and career advancement.

With luck, the ill person recovers. Recovery is a catharsis after chemotherapy; as the drugs left my body, I felt the rush of coming out of the cold and remembering what it was like to feel good. My recovery certainly had its doubts and fears, but I have never felt so ready for life's possibilities. The healing of the body can bring a healing of the mind. As much as I resented the demand that I make up for lost time, I was prepared to do so. But the caregiver's body experiences none of this. Can the pleasure she takes in watching the ill person recover give her the energy to make up for her own lost time? The person who was ill can speak of having lived through the disease; what the caregiver lived through is less easily expressed. Society has few terms to express the experience of caring, so it goes unrecognized.

But the problem is not just society. Cathie's greatest source of stress was me. She had to live each day with my fears, my obsession with this or that change in my condition, my bargaining over possible outcomes, my guilt and sense of rejection. Many of these problems were imposed on me, but the point is that they all came down on Cathie. Even she could be overpowered by my needs. It can be harder for the ill person to hold on to those who want to affirm than to ignore those who deny.

Being a caregiver is doubtless an opportunity, but the dangers of losing herself, her energies and appetites, and her sense of a future may be even greater for the caregiver than for the ill person. As little as we know of illness, we know even less of care. As much as the ill person's experience is denied, the caregiver's experience is denied more completely.

My good luck was to have a wife who was willing to be a caregiver. Together we sought to affirm the values of illness and caring that others, and sometimes even we ourselves, denied.

Comforters and Accusers

IN THE BIBLE, after Job has lost all his possessions, his children have been killed, and his skin has been covered "with sore boils from the sole of his foot unto his crown," his wife gets angry. "Curse God, and die," she tells him. Job refuses anger: "Shall we receive good at the hand of God, and shall we not receive evil?" he replies. If Job talked that way today, and if his misfortunes included cancer, he would be told he had a typical cancer personality.

Throughout this century theories have been advanced that the feelings people suppress, such as anger, cause them to have cancer. In the 1930s the poet W. H. Auden wrote a poem about Miss Gee, whose doctor attributed her cancer to childlessness and sexual repression. In the 1980s novelist Norman Mailer's fictional hero claimed he got cancer because one day he wasn't tough enough to keep chasing a gangster who had shot him. Cancer began the day he gave up on a fight, and it went into remission when he colluded in the murder of some other bad guys. Most of today's self-help authors are more subtle than Auden or Mailer, but they make the same claim that attitude causes cancer. Job's unwillingness to express his anger, to curse God, would be a prime example of someone whose personality caused cancer.

The specific makeup of the cancer personality varies. Sometimes it is based on too little sex or anger, other times on too much fear or frustration. For the last decade the suppression of anger has been more popular than sexual repression. Descriptions of cancer personalities are like horoscopes — broad enough to fit anyone, but just specific enough to allow individuals to believe their own lives are being described.

After Job's wife leaves him, he is visited by three friends whom he calls, with increasing irony, his comforters. Their comfort consists of blaming Job for having caused his own suffering. Sometimes this blame is subtle; other times it is overt: "If only you had directed your heart rightly and spread out your hands in prayer to him!" Job's friends appear as comforters, but they are really accusers. I understand them as extensions of Satan, who makes the wager with God to torment Job and see if he will renounce God. Recently "Satan" has been translated as "the Adversary" and "the Accuser."

Those who tell persons with cancer that their disease is caused by their personalities present themselves as comforters, but they too are accusers. The misfortune of getting cancer frightens people today as much as Job, who represented the complete reversal of fortune, frightened people in biblical times. Like the suddenness of Job's misfortunes, cancer represents how quickly lives can fall apart. We all fear that possibility; we want to be able to believe that we can avoid it, so we, like Job's accusers, blame it on the ill person. And we too call that blame comfort: cancer personality theories are presented as "self-help."

Society has always had personality theories to explain the

diseases it feared and did not understand. In one of the most sensible books ever written about cancer, *Illness as Metaphor*, Susan Sontag traces the history of such thinking to medieval times, when it was believed that happy people would not die of plague. We cannot prevent cancer any more than they could prevent plague, and we fear it as much. They claimed happiness was protection; we say people who do not repress anger or sex — or whatever is in fashion — will not get cancer.

We should find it funny when Sontag describes the ideas of the early psychoanalyst Wilhelm Reich, who wrote that Freud got cancer of the jaw because he repressed what he wanted to say. Because his repression involved speaking, his cancer was in the jaw. Auden placed Miss Gee's cancer, based on sexual repression, in her ovaries. But this kind of thinking is not funny, because it continues today.

A friend told me she had heard that breast cancer, which she had, was caused by problems in mother-daughter relationships. It was painful for her to think that her actions, with both her mother and her daughter, had caused her cancer. She turned the cancer personality into her own guilt, but the theory can be used against others. A woman told me that her boyfriend blamed the strains in their relationship for his cancer. Spouses or lovers may not always be supportive of someone who has cancer, but they do not cause it. Mothers may pass on a real genetic risk to their daughters, but again, relationships are not part of this risk.

When Job's accusers made him responsible for his misfortunes, they protected themselves from thinking that what had happened to him could happen to them. They, being righteous, would never end as Job had. Today the healthy want to believe that disease does not "just happen." They want to believe that they control their health and that they have earned it. Those who have cancer must have done something wrong, which the healthy can then avoid. The sick person must have participated in sickness by choosing to have a cancer personality. Otherwise illness is an intolerable reminder of how risky life is.

A friend called recently for advice about a man she knows who had just been diagnosed as having testicular cancer. She emphasized that until the diagnosis he had been absolutely fine. I wanted to say to her, Of course he was fine, disease does not always send early warning notices. But there was no need right then to remind her how fragile her world is. She is aware of that fragility in principle, but she is still shocked when a crack suddenly appears before her. Too many people find it easy to mend that crack by blaming its cause on the ill person. If we believe that the ill person has a cancer personality, then the world is less fragile, less risky, for everyone else. Even many ill people would rather believe they have done something wrong than believe disease just happened to them; guilt may be preferable to uncertainty.

For those who want to believe in a cancer personality, suppression of anger is an easy category to fit patients' behaviors into. Suppressed anger does not cause cancer, but being treated for cancer often requires the suppression of anger. One day I was lying in day care, waiting for blood results to come back from the lab. On the other side of the treatment area a physician was talking loudly with a volunteer, discussing vacation spots in the Caribbean, specifically, which side of some island was the rainy side. This was not a conversation I or the others having chemotherapy wanted to hear. Most of us were worried about getting through the day's treatment without having a vein collapse. We were wondering if we would ever leave Calgary again, much less get to a place like the Caribbean. Physicians need vacations, but these two never considered how they sounded to others; they failed to recognize what ill persons are living through.

In a chemotherapy unit, their talk was an appropriate object for anger. But Cathie and I kept our anger to ourselves, just as we had concealed our anger toward the physicians who misdiagnosed me. We grumbled only to ourselves because I was dependent on the treatment facility, and we were making our best deal.

Whether in treatment or at home, ill persons rarely perceive expressing anger as part of the best deal. Dependence is the primary fact of illness, and ill persons act with more or less fear of offending those they depend on. It seems like a bad deal to express anger at someone who may soon be approaching your body with sharp pointed instruments or, if offended, may be slow to bring a bedpan, or who may be the only person one can say goodnight to. Patients who do express anger usually believe they have little left to lose; the situation and the disease have already done their worst.

I did not need to have cancer to find myself in situations that made me angry. But when my treatment for cancer depended on suppressing my anger, when it was a matter of life and death, then the suppression was particularly bitter. And only as a person with cancer was I told that "my" suppression of anger had caused the disease in the first place.

Cancer personality theories will persist, because they have a payoff for everyone. On the one hand the ill person is accused, but on the other she is comforted. Perhaps by changing her personality she can recover; it is never too late. Those around the ill person can rest assured that he got cancer because he was that sort of person, different from themselves. Society as a whole can continue to perpetuate conditions and behaviors that increase the risks of cancer while blaming its incidence on the personalities of individuals. We can smoke, pollute, expose ourselves to radiation, use unsafe food additives, destroy the ozone layer, consume high levels of fat, take inadequately tested prescription drugs, make work more stressful, have an educational and occupational system that encourages delayed childbearing, fail to require retraining of physicians who make wrong diagnoses — but we still talk about causes of cancer in terms of individual personality.

The genius of the cancer personality argument is that it means nothing has to change. The fault and the fear are safely contained, locked up inside the cancer patient. Cigarette companies stay in business, polluters can pollute, advertisers can glorify sunbathing, and those who enjoy good health can believe they have earned it. Only the ill are left to feel guilty.

After Job has dismissed the arguments of his accusers, God answers him. The answer to his misfortune is that he has no right to ask. Job learns that his misfortunes are nothing more than part of his humanity. Job's final words, in Stephen Mitchell's translation, are, "Therefore I will be quiet, comforted that I am dust." Cancer is no god, but the person with cancer can find in Job's story a kind of answer and comfort. Disease is part of the dust of our bodies; we accept it when we accept life. It is our humanity to contest disease as long as we can, but it is also our humanity to die.

That is an answer to disease; illness is another problem.

One of the real tragedies of cancer is that so much anger is kept quiet. If expressed and responded to, this anger would make the world a better place. Having cancer taught me how many of the actions of individuals, institutions, and society are simply not decent ways to behave. When I was ill I expressed little of this anger, not because I had a cancer personality, but because I was doing what I had to do to get by. I write now for the times I had to remain silent and for those who are still silent.

Even when we are not forced into a deal requiring us to suppress anger, finding the appropriate object for anger is not easy. People, whether physicians, manufacturers, or smokers, act within systems they did not create. Getting angry at individuals does only so much good, but it does some good. Each friend, associate, or treatment provider remains responsible for his actions. We need to be angry with individuals who treat us badly, just as we need to appreciate all the obstacles society and its institutions use to prevent us from expressing this anger. Cancer personality theory is one such obstacle; it turns people inside themselves, into their own guilt, and away from changing the society that perpetuates real risks. The cancer personality theory is the final insult by comforters who are really accusers.

Valuing Illness

PHYSICIANS and nurses, medical ethicists and philoso-
phers, economists and political scientists express opinions
about what care society owes or does not owe ill persons. As
an aging population combines with advancing medical technology, more people will need treatment, and more treatment
will be available. The question is who will get what and who
will pay. But in all that has been written, the ill themselves
have had little to say, or else no one has listened. From the
perspective of an ill person, the root issue is suffering. Is
society willing to recognize the suffering of the ill as a common
condition of humanity, and can we find value in illness? I
believe that when society learns to value the ill, the other
questions of rights — the complicated questions of payments
and technologies and treatments — will fall into place with
remarkable ease.

Seeing the question of rights from the perspective of the ill
begins with accepting the inevitability of illness. To everyone
except those who die in accidents or conflicts, a disease will
just happen someday. That fact is not popular, and those who

are not presently ill prefer to think about decreasing their risks of disease by living one way rather than another. We can decrease risks, and we should. But no amount of vitamins, proper diet, exercise, sunshine or sunscreen, relaxation, meditation, or joyful stress will change two facts: each of us will die, and most deaths will be preceded by a long or a short illness. I write this easily, based on an experience that was hard. When my mother-in-law was dying, she spent some time in the same hospital room where I had been treated not long before. It did not take much imagination to see myself in her place.

If those persons who are not presently ill could believe that disease is their inevitable fate, they might think differently about who pays for treatment. I have not mentioned costs and fees, and American readers may be puzzled by the omission. In Canada government insurance pays everyone's costs of medical care through general tax revenues. Physicians and treatment facilities remain autonomous, but instead of billing patients or insurance companies, they bill the province or receive provincial funding. The patient receives treatment just as she would in the American system, except that she gives the hospital or doctor her health-care identification number instead of making a payment. For all my treatments for heart problems and cancer, the only medical bill we paid was a fifteen-dollar-a-day surcharge for a private room I was assigned once by chance. This was later reimbursed by my university health insurance. We did pay for a small proportion of the prescription drugs I took at home to offset side effects of chemotherapy. Our only other expenses were for parking and for Cathie's meals at the hospital.

The Canadian health system is being attacked by those who complain about its expense. In fact Canada spends a lower proportion of its gross national product on health care than the United States does. The cost, however, is distributed equally among all taxpayers rather than falling disproportionately on the ill. It is this distribution that is under attack. Some of those doing the attacking may want a system that allows them to use greater personal resources to purchase more exclusive treatment; others may want to open health care to entrepreneurial profit making. Still others may deny that someday they will need treatment, and want ill persons — others — to pay for what they get.

I can imagine nothing more cruel than being forced to make my own treatment decisions based on cost. As a minor example, the nurses at day care gave us the syringes we used every day to flush my intravenous line with saline solution. They told us that in other cancer centers the decision on how often to flush the line depends on the budget for syringes, not on what is most effective for maintaining the lines. They also told us that some lines fail because they are not flushed frequently enough. Given my dependence on the line, it would have been cruel to gamble on flushing it often enough. But in a system where patients themselves pay, it would be just as cruel to think that each time you flushed the line, you were taking resources away from your family. The strains an ill person imposes on family caregivers are great enough without depriving them financially as well.

Of course, private insurance provides treatment without the ill person having to pay for it directly. But private insurance is just that, available to some but not to all. There is nothing private about having cancer; I have never shared so self-consciously in the common risk of being human. Cancer may have been all I had in common with many of those in treatment with me, but cancer defined each of our lives. Because we shared cancer, I wanted no less for them than I wanted for myself. I did not want my treatment to be a privilege based on my occupation or income. If cancer occurs without prejudice, its treatment should be available without prejudice as well.

Even when treatment is publicly funded, it remains unequal. Depending on personal income, ill persons differ in their access to good nutrition, the restfulness of their home, their ability to reduce their workload, and even recreation. The effectiveness of treatment reflects these inequalities, but treatment itself should be a high-water mark of fairness. At least those who shared my disease had access to the same treatment I had. My recovery was not bought at the cost of anyone else's lack of treatment.

The right to treatment is the beginning of recognizing the ill, but it is not yet an expression of value. Even if society provides treatment to all, it may still relegate the ill to the margins where we drop off the other "unproductive" ones — children, the handicapped, the old, the untrained. Treatment in itself is not an expression that the individual is valued; it is an investment in the ill person's future productivity. The ill are regarded as healthy people inside broken-down bodies that need fixing. The hard question is whether we can value the ill as people whose experience challenges the way the rest of us live.

The healthy can begin to value illness by doubting the standard of productivity by which they measure their lives. Although I have once again become "productive," I am not sure if I am living better or worse than I was during illness. I often wish I could live a bit more as I did then, without having to have cancer. Illness, and perhaps only illness, gives us permission to slow down. It took a disease as devastating as cancer to allow me simply to sit and watch the afternoon light and finally think seriously about that picture of Jacob I had merely looked at for sixteen years.

I often think I have not yet been ill enough to know how to live. I still evaluate choices in terms of what counts on my résumé, instead of asking whether I am producing something I think is valuable and if I am meeting people's needs rather than fulfilling the demands of some system. I still feel threatened by the disease and the suffering of others. The threat is not only that I might become like them again, but that I might have to stop and care for someone else. I fear not only suffering but slowing down. It is natural to fear suffering; to fear slowing down is deranged. But all around me I see people afraid of slowing down, fearful of offending the production machines we work for.

Several years after chemotherapy, I now find myself resenting the time I spend on tasks I wanted so much to do, but lacked the strength for, when I was ill. I take my senses for granted, and I miss the joy I felt from suddenly hearing music or taking a walk or being in my own home and sleeping through the night. When I was ill I valued just being with others. Too often now I think of people as intruding on my work. I forget to ask myself if what I'm doing is so terribly important that I should allow it to crowd out all else.

Instead of setting the healthy and the ill apart, we should think about the rights of the living. Among the basic rights that should belong to every human is that of experiencing what is happening to oneself. We are so rushed from moment to moment that we are unable to reflect on what we are becoming. We spend our lives learning to be productive, to use our bodies as instruments of production. Whether we work at a computer terminal or on an assembly line or in a home, we know exactly what it means to use the body as an instrument of production. We know very little of what it means to be productive *of* ourselves, but this sort of production should be our basic human right.

To understand what the rights of the ill mean, we must ask what is required to produce one's self as a human being. This kind of production first requires care from others, and then it requires time, space, basic comforts, and some level of aesthetic choice. Ultimately it requires that the conditions of our lives enable us to return to others something of the care we have received. All this is necessary if we are to experience life rather than just survive it. None of these rights should be anything special.

The ultimate value of illness is that it teaches us the value of being alive; this is why the ill are not just charity cases, but a presence to be valued. Illness and, ultimately, death remind us of living. "The way we look to a distant constellation / That's dying in a corner of the sky," Paul Simon sang. We look like a flicker of light. In the moment of that light going out, we learn that what counts is to keep it burning. Death is no enemy of life; it restores our sense of the value of living. Illness restores the sense of proportion that is lost when we take life for granted. To learn about value and proportion we need to honor illness, and ultimately to honor death.

When my mother-in-law was dying, I found visiting her hard work. Cancer wards are not pleasant places, whether you bring the memories of an ex-patient or the anticipations of a possible future one. The demands of a working life provide easy excuses to stay away. But my mother-in-law had a right to the time of anyone she wanted to have around her. I had learned why when I lay in those same beds. Seeing the world from a bed in a cancer ward is like seeing it from outer space: it is rather small and fundamentally whole. To be ill, to share in the suffering of being human is to know your place in that whole, to know your connection with others. For the person who is dying, being with others expresses that connection, which alone has value and restores proportion.

My mother-in-law had no choice but to stay in that hospital, immobilized by breast, liver, and bone cancer, and experience her life running out. She had every right to whatever connection I could provide, but I had no less a right to my time with her. All I ever needed to learn about life was at her bedside in those days, shared in hearing her last words and watching the final struggles of her body. When our visits, and then her life, were over, I was able to walk outside under a blue or a starry sky, breathe real air, and know how we look to a distant constellation.

The rights of the ill resolve into the simplest questions. What is the core of experience that binds us together as human? If the answer includes suffering, then do we each, as individuals, have the strength to recognize our own place in that suffering? If we can recognize it, how do we honor it? These questions lead to the most practical ends: Is there any better reason to tax ourselves than for health care? What else do we have to do with our time than spend it with loved ones who are dying? The most practical question of all is how we can become productive of ourselves as human beings. We begin by witnessing the suffering of illness, sharing it, and allowing ourselves to live in the light of what that sharing teaches us we can be.

Listening to the Ill

ILLNESS excuses people from their normal responsibilities, but the cost of being excused is greater than it appears at first. An excuse is also an exclusion. When an ill person is told, "All you have to do is get well," he is also being told that all he *can* do is be ill. Telling someone he doesn't have to do anything but get well turns into a message that he has no right to do anything until he can return to his normal tasks. Again, just being ill has no value; on the contrary, the ill person is culpable.

People can't give up the idea that the ill person is responsible for the disease. If the ill person has a responsibility to get well, then presumably he is responsible for having become ill in the first place. The ideal of getting well also excludes and devalues those who will not get well.

If we reject the notion that the ill are responsible for getting well, then what *is* their responsibility? It is to witness their own suffering and to express this experience so that the rest of us can learn from it. Of course others must be willing to learn; society's reciprocal responsibility is to see and hear what ill people express.

A recent newspaper story suggests how little we understand about the expression of experience as both a right and a responsibility. The story's theme is the need for cancer patients to "talk openly" about their illness. This need is defined as exclusively the patient's; the story does not mention society's need to hear such talk or whether others are willing to listen. The story, a medical-psychological moral fable, contrasts two teenagers with leukemia. One teenager exemplifies openness. When a stranger in a supermarket asks her if she is ill, she raises her wig and says that she is being treated for leukemia. The other teenager withdraws from friends and physicians and refuses further treatment. Without saying so, the article implies that the "open" child will survive and the "withdrawn" child will not.

Stories like this perform a sleight of hand; they make the social context of each child's life disappear. Each teenager has a history of relationships with other people, and it is this history that produces the different behaviors. Their responses to leukemia do not just happen, the way some of us just happen to get leukemia. Whatever causes the disease, the response to it is learned. The teenagers' openness and withdrawal are responses to their experiences with family, friends, schools, and medical staff. The "open" one has been lucky enough to feel valued regardless of being ill. Her sense of stigma at home, at school, and in the hospital has been minimized. She has been allowed to feel that whatever problems her disease creates, illness is not a personal failure. She takes a risk when she shows her bald head to a stranger, but her willingness to do so results from how those around her have already responded to her baldness. The people she has met have acted in ways that allow her to anticipate support from those she now meets; at least she knows she has people to fall back on.

An ill child withdraws when he senses that people do not like what he represents. To his parents he embodies their failure to have a healthy child. He sees them being sad and guilty, and he feels guilty for having made them feel this way. To his siblings he may represent a drain on family time and financial resources. To other children his presence brings a fear of something they understand only enough to worry that it will happen to them. All adolescents experience their bodies changing, and his peers may see in the leukemic their fears of these changes gone wrong. To medical staff he represents their failure to cure him. I imagine his physicians evaluate their professional self-image in terms of the success of their treatments. They see themselves in a contest with the disease, and when disease persists, they have lost. They cannot think in terms of care that goes beyond treatment.

The child withdraws because he believes others would be happier if they did not have to see him. They may not reject him in any overt way, but he senses from their expressions that he is causing them pain. His withdrawal is no more the result of his "personality" (much less the lack of what some call "fighting spirit") than the other child's openness is. Each child is only looking around, assessing what support is available, and making what seems to be the best deal.

The newspaper story does not talk about the children's circumstances; instead it discusses withdrawal as "psychologically damaging" and openness as being "better adjusted." But the children are not damaged or adjusted; society is. The social group around each child has either helped her adjust or has damaged him, and those groups in turn find support or denial in other groups. The newspaper story makes these groups disappear through its use of the word "psychological," creating the illusion that each child's behavior comes out of that child, the way the leukemia comes from within the child's physiology. Healthy people comfortably accept the social myth that illness behavior is inside the person. We want to enclose the ill person in a psychological language that turns his reality inward, closing it off to external influence. Then we hand the whole thing over to medicine.

The ultimate moral of the story is medical compliance. The open child is the good medical citizen who stays in treatment. The withdrawn child plays his sick role badly. He does not try to get well. As soon as we think of the child's withdrawal as "his" and not a response learned from others, we cannot avoid the implication that he does not deserve to get well. Although the story quotes physicians and passes itself off as "scientific," the science only dresses up the moral fable beneath. The disease is depicted as a fall from the grace of a normal childhood. One child redeems herself through the courage of her openness, and the other continues falling. By making disease an issue of the ill person's morality, the story perpetuates a language of stigma.

Where is responsibility in this story? The newspaper account carries a clear implication that the ill person's responsibility is to be a good medical citizen. But the matter is not so simple. I see the children as equally responsible, though only one is happily so. The happy child lifts her wig and proclaims she is a leukemia patient. She performs a significant act of public education, and I have no wish to detract from the honor she deserves. I hope the person she spoke to came away recognizing the ill person's strength as a person, not just a patient. When she perpetuates the openness she has experienced from others, the child widens the circle of public recognition. She has fulfilled her responsibility.

But the withdrawn child is no less responsible, no less a witness to his experience. Like the open child, he reflects the attitudes of those around him. He too acts according to others' cues of what they want of him, which is to disappear. His withdrawal may result in psychological damage, but again the initial damage is not the child's. The damage is caused by those who cannot value the ill.

We may talk about the heroic individual who puts aside society's script for illness, but this is mostly just talk. Even the ill person who refuses to let her actions be determined by the way she is treated bases this response on resources developed earlier. Adolescents are more susceptible to the way they are treated at the moment because their personal history is shorter. We who are older are no less creatures of the ways we have been treated; we just have a longer history against which to evaluate our present circumstances.

The responsibility of the ill, then, is not to get well but to express their illness well. And the two have nothing to do with each other. I wish I could believe that those who express their illness well have a greater chance of recovery, but I cannot. Perhaps someday we will understand more of how the mind affects the body. For now I only believe that those who express their illness live their lives fully to the end of the illness. For me this is enough — it has to be enough. If we cannot value life for itself, then we see ill persons only in terms of what they could be doing if they were well, and we see children only as what they will do when they become adults. We fail to value life as a frail bit of good luck in a world based on chance. The ill have already fulfilled their responsibility by being ill. The question is whether the rest of us can be responsible enough to see and hear what illness is, which ultimately means seeing and hearing what life is. Being alive is a dual responsibility: to our shared frailty, on the one hand, and to all we can create, on the other. The mutual responsibilities of the ill to express and the healthy to hear meet in the recognition that our creativity depends on our frailty. Life without illness would not just be incomplete, it would be impossible. The paradox is that illness must remain painful, even to those who fully believe its necessity.

The most painful sight we ever confront is that of beauty yielding to impermanence. Of our creations, we may consider children the most beautiful. When they reveal their frail impermanence by becoming critically ill, it is painful to remain open to that illness. In children most of all we want to deny illness. We want to withdraw into an illusion of permanence, that children will turn into adults, and we will not have to see them die. But that illusion is another sleight of hand in which life, the creative frailty and the frail creativity, disappears.

Ceremonies of Recovery

RECOVERY deserves a ceremony. Many aboriginal peoples have reentry rituals during which a person who has been stigmatized is purified. These rituals are a rebirth; afterward life can begin anew. Each of my critical illnesses ended with a medical event that could have been given a ritual value. But physicians, the high priests of our time, have let themselves be reduced to mere medical technicians. They act as if they are unaware of the power of their interventions to change the body's symbolic value. Both the patient and physician are thus deprived of the spiritual experience of illness. Because ritual self-awareness is excluded from the system, it takes longer to work out one's own terms of reentry.

The angiogram which showed that my heart problems were over had ritual potential, and I had the sense to value the sight of my own heart beating. But medicine reduced the angiogram to the end of an incident. I accepted, even embraced, this reduction and did not try to experience it as the beginning of a life that was now different. The angiogram only signaled the end of a breakdown; it was not an occasion for rebirth.

After the angiogram I could believe that the incident was over. There had been a virus, but now it was gone. I had no more heart problems, period. After cancer, however, I had no such belief. Cancer never disappears. I read recently about a young man whose cancer recurred after a thirteen-year remission. Medical science is just beginning to understand cancer's capacity to be present in the body but inactive for decades. Cancer creates the disturbing image of the body as a time bomb, genetically programmed to explode at some future time. I could be having a recurrence now and not yet know it, or I could live another forty years and die of something else. You are never cured of cancer; you can only live in remission.

My remission began several weeks after the third round of chemotherapy. The CAT scan showed that the tumors had shrunk, but the reduction was no longer considerable. The remaining masses on the X-rays were assumed to be scar tissue, which would never disappear entirely but would continue to reduce gradually. The chemotherapy was judged to have done what it could. My treatment could end.

My intravenous line provided its last valuable service as the occasion of a ceremony. After reporting the scan, the physician left Cathie and me in a treatment cubicle while he prepared another room for the surgical procedure of pulling out the line. Its installation had changed our relationship by requiring each of our days to begin and end with a focus on cancer. The care of the line had tied Cathie to me and tied us both to cancer; these ties had brought nuisance and caring, fear and possibility. Because of the line's symbolism, as well as its problems, we had looked forward to its removal as the beginning of life after cancer. My own emotions were intensified by the physical drain of preparing for the scan. I had not eaten in about twenty-four hours and had had almost no sleep. My physical reserves and our emotional reserves were gone, so we started to cry, in a mixture of joy, relief, and just plain breakdown.

When a nurse came into the room and saw us crying, she looked totally confused. Suddenly a light bulb went on. "I guess this must be kind of a big moment for you," she said. She was a good nurse and had been mercifully quick and efficient at getting prescriptions to manage painful side effects, but for her, suffering was a problem of management, not a crisis of spirit. Her perceptions were always on the surface of bodies. That moment was one of the few times she saw beyond the disease to the experience of illness. She talked happily of former patients returning to see her when their hair had grown back; chemotherapy sounded like a problem of grooming. When hair returns, all is forgotten. But when all is forgotten, nothing is learned. Her way of seeing missed the ritual, which is a passage through real and symbolic dangers in preparation for the opportunity of a life enhanced by that passage.

The line was pulled, the incision sewed up. Medicine, as ritual, inflicted another mark on my body, giving that body a value it did not have before. Ritual markings are not just stigmas; scarification during an initiation rite marks the person as having passed through some level of experience, entitling him to higher status as a result. Thus initiated, my body was mine again. Life could begin once more. Of course I knew life had never stopped. The nights listening to Bach, the afternoon light on the Chagall print, the moments of hope and fear shared with Cathie, the losses and frustrations had been

anything but life stopping during cancer. It had only intensified. If the months from the ultrasound in September to the
removal of the line in January seemed like a lifetime, it was
because during this time everything counted. I could not afford to let anything slip by unobserved and unfelt.

My life had not stopped, but a great deal of it had been put
on hold. Now I could begin to make plans again, to think of
travel, to commit myself to projects at work. The process of
reentry was not smooth. I now knew that the way I and others lived was a choice, and often not the best one. My consciousness remained suspended between the insulated world
of illness and the "healthy" mainstream. This suspension expressed itself in my lack of tolerance for tension and disagreements. I continued to value much of the life of an ill person,
even though I was no longer officially diseased.

I still needed time to myself. It was warm in Calgary that
winter, and I took long walks on the hills overlooking the
river. I chose the time for these walks so that I would come
over the crest of the hill just as the afternoon sun shone
directly on the water. Chemotherapy had deprived me of air
and sun. I wanted to store up these elements against the
possibility that I might be deprived of them again. In that
sunlight on the river I began to heal.

I become less and less a person with cancer, but the continuing schedule of examinations, X-rays, and blood tests
reminds me that I remain at greater risk than others. This risk
diminishes over time but never disappears. Life remains a
remission. But my sense of being a person with cancer is on the
level of experience, not of medicine. I do not want to take
recovery too far. Part of the fear of dying is realizing all that

I have not done or have not done enough of. As long as life remains a recovery, I try to seize the life I someday want to have lived. The value of remaining a person with cancer is to keep asking the question: If I get sick again, what will I tell myself about the way I spent my time?

I am also reminded of cancer when I meet people I see infrequently. Some ask, guardedly, how my health is. Their concern recognizes that cancer is never "over" in the way a virus is over when it passes out of the body. Others greet me by pronouncing, "You're fine." Theirs is less a question than a statement. I hear their wish that cancer never happens, and, if it has to happen, that it be put away. I have assumed a dual presence for people. My being here suggests that cancer is not always fatal, but that it does happen. Some see the survival in the foreground and the risk in the background; for others the risk dominates. On different days I myself emphasize different halves.

I am trying, in this third year after cancer, to be a little less afraid. Some days the world seems immensely fearful, a place where some germ cell is waiting to explode. Another of Paul Simon's memorable lyrics says, "Somebody could walk into this room / And say your life is on fire." One day during a self-examination I felt something I had not felt in the two years since surgery. I panicked but made an appointment to see the same urologist who had originally diagnosed me. A few days later Cathie and I were again waiting in a treatment ward, listening to the other patients through the thin curtains. We sat there waiting for the urologist, who could walk into that room and say our lives were on fire. But it did not happen that time. Whatever it was I had noticed, he pronounced me normal. We left, less happy than dazed by the vision of what might have happened. This vision gives each day its value. Of course the condition of my life is no different from anyone else's, but I get these reminders, for which I am grateful.

The only real difference between people is not health or illness but the way each holds onto a sense of value in life. When I feel I have no time to walk out and watch the sunlight on the river, my recovery has gone too far. A little fear is all right. It is all right to know that in a month I could be lying in a hospital bed asking myself how I spent today. Holding onto that question — how did you spend today? — reminds me to feel and see and hear. It is too easy to become distracted. When the ordinary becomes frustrating, I have to remember those times when the ordinary was forbidden to me. When I was ill, all I wanted was to get back into the ordinary flux of activity. Now that I am back in the ordinary, I have to retain a sense of wonder at being here.

Like Job, I have had my goods restored to me. Secure in the knowledge that I am dust, I enjoy what I have. I even run again, not as far or as fast, but with greater pleasure. Long runs let my mind drift to whatever fantasy comes along. Some days that fantasy turns to my death, but not in sadness. I wonder what kind of death I would need, to feel I had lived well. What I tell myself changes; all that matters is staying at peace with my own mortality.

I want to keep running, but someday I will have to stop. I do not know what that day will be like. If I have recovered well but not too much, I will remember a poem I keep over my desk by the late Raymond Carver, called "Gravy." A man, an alcoholic, is about to die, but he changes his habits and lives for ten years. Then he gets a brain disease and again is dying. He tells his friends not to mourn:

"I've had ten years longer than I or anyone expected. Pure gravy. And don't you forget it."

I try not to.

When I become ill again, and someday I will, I hope it will not be the total break in my life, the radical discontinuity, that I experienced before. Health and illness are not so different. In the best moments of my illnesses I have been most whole. In the worst moments of my health I am sick. Where should I live? Health and illness, wellness and sickness perpetually alternate as foreground and background. Each exists only because of the other and can only alternate with its other. There is no rest in either word. In "health" there can only be fear of illness, and in "illness" there is only discontent at not being healthy. In recovery I seek not health but a word that has no opposite, a word that just is, in itself. When I seek the meaning of my recovery, the opportunity of illness, I call it gravy.

Gravy

I BEGAN THINKING about the experience of illness when I recognized something of my own situation in the picture of Jacob wrestling with the angel. I can end my story with this morning's "Far Side" cartoon. A bearded man stands at the front door, dripping wet, in rags. The woman opening the door says, "For crying out loud, Jonah! Three days late, covered with slime, and smelling like a fish! . . . And what story have I got to swallow this time?" Like Jonah, I have been spit back into life by the great fish of illness. The story I have been asking you to swallow is almost over.

Our lives are attempts to make sense of what we are living through. Self-reflection is our curse and our possibility. I have suggested that illness is an opportunity for self-reflection of a kind not otherwise available. This opportunity has its dangers, not the least of which is romanticizing illness. We need to think about illness, but too much thinking can turn it into something it is not. Illness is not any kind of enlightenment. Illness is nothing more than the body moving on. My body was moving too rapidly toward death. Surgery and chemicals

restored that movement to its normal pace, sort of. Some part
of me still knows where it was going. I wait to finish the
journey my body now knows is inescapable. I hope to wait a
long time, but not forever.

I have written little of death because I have little to say. At
the same time I was diagnosed as having cancer, a good friend
my age was also diagnosed, and my mother-in-law came out
of remission again. They both have died. I can make no sense
of their deaths and my survival. Some people who have lived
through cancer attribute their survival to some act of will.
They speak of choosing to live and of the mind willing the
body back to health. They mean well, and their belief may
bring comfort to some. But when I think of the real people
who are now dead, and wonder why I live, the idea that I
chose to live and they did not seems presumptuous at best and
obscene at worst. Disease just happened to them in the same
way it just happened to me. It just happened to happen differently.

Sometimes I feel very strange, just being alive. It's a comfortable strangeness, but strange nonetheless. My body seems
to know in some way that it should not be living. Just as my
body remembers the moment of death during my heart attack,
it knows it was dying of cancer and cannot figure out what
stopped the process. I happened to get cancer, and then I
happened to respond to a treatment that happened to be
available. That's the strangeness of contingency: neither my
body nor my mind knows why these things happened as they
did. As I remake my place in this life, it too seems to have just
happened, to be a contingency.

But if disease just happens, where does choice fit in? People who have died are often described as "cancer victims." This phrase has a certain accuracy, but it eliminates the choice that was also theirs. The word "victim" is a half-truth. We may be victims of disease, but we are not victims of illness. Individuals can do little to prevent certain diseases. If many people choose to act in certain ways, those choices, spread across a population, will change the total incidence of disease. Such action matters when we consider a whole society, but for any individual, odds are only odds. Some of those with the lowest risk factors will still get sick, and in some sense, though only in part, they will be victims.

Choice becomes possible when we shift the perspective from the disease to the illness. Because we can choose how we experience illness, we can be more than victims. Choice can turn the worst of circumstances into an experience of value. But choices are limited. The care I received was my good luck, not my choice. We can choose only from what is available. We are not victims of circumstances, but circumstances limit our choices. The idea of choice is another half-truth. The trick is to hold onto the half that is true.

I used to think of activities like running and writing as choices. Then cancer prevented me from doing them, and I decided they were gifts. But gifts imply a giver. Now I think that much of what happens just happens. One day you run twenty miles and the next you have a heart attack. The gift is our human capacity to choose how we use each day, however limited our choices.

Half-victims making half-choices are my fellow citizens in the remission society. I began to think of myself as living in the "remission society" when I realized the ordinariness of my experience of illness. As I write and talk about illness, people tell me about living in some kind of remission, many from cancer, others from equally debilitating diseases. My history is nothing special.

The remission society is new. Disease used to be either critical, meaning life-threatening but quick, or chronic, meaning long-term. Disease moved to a crisis from which the patient either recovered or died, or else the patient lived as an invalid, gradually wasting away. Medical technology keeps enlarging the numbers of those living "normally" in remission; we have more and more of the "chronically critical." They go about their business with alternating periods of activity and treatment. Life for them is remission, as it is for their caregivers. By choosing to tie their lives to the illness of others, caregivers too see life as a kind of remission. They too know that somebody could walk into the room and say their lives are on fire.

What is life like in the remission society? For me it is ordinary or everyday, a quality so simple and so everpresent that it becomes difficult to describe. The quality of light in a room is everyday, as is the smell of the air. Being among people is ordinary; so are clothes we like, food we enjoy, and the fit of a body into a comfortable chair, the touch of other bodies. These details make up any life. People in the remission society notice details more, because illness teaches the value as well as the danger of the everyday.

The danger is that ordinary discomforts will persist and accumulate. I have written of many discomforts that in the course of a healthy life would be no more than annoying: morning blood tests in the hospital, strong laxatives before

CAT scans, and even any single side effect of chemotherapy. But as these mundane discomforts accumulate, they take over everyday life. They become all an ill person has to look forward to. And one day, after many days with nothing else to look forward to, that person changes. She doesn't decide to change or even perceive that she has changed, but she has. She has been worn away, and she doesn't care anymore. Among caregivers this change is called burnout. Ill persons also burn out. Some may continue in treatment, but only because they don't care enough to stop. Those who do stop treatment are the ones who still care about how they live; they are willing to live a shorter time, under circumstances they hope will be more of their own choosing. The burned-out ones have given up caring. They keep going but are only waiting for the end.

But living among the everyday is also the opportunity of illness, which brings me back to gravy. Gravy is beyond health or illness, beyond the desire for health, which necessarily brings the fear of the illness. Gravy does not romanticize illness but is willing to accept it for what it can bring.

Gravy is watching the sunlight on the river. Here is half of what I have learned from illness:

> Sky is blue,
> Water sparkles.

This verse is only half. Watching the sunlight remains solitary. The other half of life's joys are with others, in pleasure and in pain. These halves become a whole. To be able to recognize the pain of others, to witness life's sufferings, we need some grounding in what is our own. My grounding is, Sky is blue, Water sparkles. From there I can begin to reach out.

The world I reach out to is a world in which I see myself. That was what I saw that night, early in my cancer, when I was in such pain. In that frosted window I saw myself. Not the self I see in a mirror, but a world I am so completely a part of that it too is myself. The sight allowed me to exist outside my body's pain and at the same time to see why that pain was part of the same world as the window, as necessary to that world as the window's beauty was. The lesson I learned looking into that frosted window was expressed centuries ago in the Chinese holy book, the *Tao Te Ching*:

> See the world as your self.
> Have faith in the way things are.
> Love the world as your self;
> then you can care for all things.

When I can care for the sunlight on the river enough to imagine that it will be there without me, when I have faith in its being there, then my self rests in a world beyond itself and I am no longer afraid to die. When I can see the faces of those I love smiling after I am gone, then I can take pleasure in being here. But I do not have to be here; my pleasure is knowing I can let go.

So the sun rises on another day in the remission society. It rises on a world that is everyday, in all its opportunity and danger. It rises on a day when some will be victims, and all will make choices, though some will have more scope for choice than others. In the remission society all struggle to be responsible, but only some will be granted the rights necessary to act in ways that enhance their lives. Many will experience stigma, a few will know it for what it is, and even fewer will be able to overcome how it makes them feel. Some will express anger, bits of which will find their proper target and lead someone else to change. Ill persons will be denied and will find care. Some will lie in rooms where they cannot see the sun, and others will find themselves at home, able to value it as they never have. Some will burn out; others will prevail.

How strange and wonderful the world must have looked to Jonah, come out of the belly of that great fish. Could he preserve the poignancy of that first moment, after three days in the slime and the stink, when he saw the light and land and water, and knew the face of God?

Throughout this book I have minimized the use of quotations and references to others' writings. But ideas do not derive from personal experience alone, and acknowledgment of works I have drawn on directly is due. Susan Sontag's *Illness as Metaphor* (Farrar, Straus and Giroux, 1978) taught me how careful ill persons must be in describing their illnesses, as well as in accepting descriptions from others. Arthur Kleinman's *The Illness Narratives* (Basic Books, 1988) affirmed the value of witnessing suffering. At a time when I was wondering whether to write this book, Kleinman's book showed me why ill persons need to express what they are going through, both for themselves and for the healthy.

My models of accounts by ill persons included two works by other social scientists: Irving Zola's *Missing Pieces* (Temple University Press, 1982) and Robert F. Murphy's *The Body Silent* (Henry Holt, 1987). Oliver Sacks's *A Leg to Stand On* (Harper & Row, 1984), Nan Shin's *Diary of a Zen Nun: Every Day Living* (E. P. Dutton, 1986), and John Updike's essay "At War with My Skin," in *Self-Consciousness: Mem-*

oirs (Ballantine, 1989), contained further lessons both on how to live with illness and how to turn it into narratiave.

Although this book is not a work of sociology, I owe debts in that field also. Few nonspecialists may want to attempt the writings of Talcott Parsons, but his conception of "the sick role" has led me into my most productive disagreements. Parsons wrote about sickness in various books, from *The Social System* (Free Press, 1951) to *Action Theory and the Human Condition* (Free Press, 1978). Arlie Hochschild does not write about illness in *The Managed Heart* (University of California Press, 1983), but this book gave me a vocabulary to express my ideas about how ill persons are supposed to sustain an appearance acceptable to others. The one sociology book I would recommend to anyone is Erving Goffman's *Stigma* (Prentice Hall, 1963). Although Goffman says little if anything about cancer, his discussion of other "spoiled identities" applies in varying degrees to all ill persons.

Illness, as I have tried to write, presents us with many windows and mirrors. What I saw in them was affected most by works of poetry and spirituality. The writings of the Zen master D. T. Suzuki have informed my thinking thoughout. I also owe a singular debt to Stephen Mitchell for his translations of Rainer Maria Rilke's *Letters to a Young Poet* (Random House, 1984), the *Tao Te Ching* (Harper & Row, 1988), and *The Book of Job* (North Point Press, 1987), as well as his own commentaries and poetry. Compared to what these writings offer, what I have learned is nothing. But part of what they teach me is not to fear beginnings.